D1515931

From Zip Lines to Hosaphones

From Zip Lines to Hosaphones

Dispatches from the Search
for Truth and Meaning

Jane Ranney Rzepka

Skinner House Books
Boston

Printed in the United States

Cover and text design by Suzanne Morgan

print ISBN: 978-1-55896-617-8   eBook ISBN: 978-1-55896-618-5

6 5 4 3 2 1 / 14 13 12 11

Library of Congress Cataloging-in-Publication Data

Rzepka, Jane Ranney, 1950-
  From zip lines to hosaphones : dispatches from the search for truth and meaning / Jane Ranney Rzepka.
      p. cm.
  ISBN 978-1-55896-617-8 (pbk. : alk. paper) — ISBN 978-1-55896-618-5 (ebook)
  1. Meditations. 2. Unitarian Universalist Association—Sermons. 3. Sermons, American—21st century. I. Title.
  BX9855.R94 2011
  252'.09132—dc22

                         2011006463

"Playing with Three Strings" from *Finding Each Other in Judaism* by Harold M. Schulweis, copyright © 2001 by the UAHC Press, reprinted with permission of URJ Press; excerpt from "Theatre Impressions" from *View With a Grain of Sand*, copyright © 1993 by Wislawa Szymborska, English translation by Stanislaw Baranczak and Clare Cavanagh copyright © 1995 by Houghton Mifflin Harcourt Publishing Company, reprinted by permission of the publisher; excerpt from "Love after Love" from *Collected Poems 1948–1984* by Derek Walcott, copyright © 1986 by Derek Walcott, reprinted by permission of Farrar, Straus and Giroux, LLC; "The Whistler" from *Winter Hours: Prose, Prose Poems and Poems by Mary Oliver*, copyright © 1999 by Mary Oliver, reprinted by permission of Houghton Mifflin Harcourt Publishing Company, all rights reserved; "Wild Geese" from *Dream Work*, copyright © 1986 by Mary Oliver, used by permission of Grove/Atlantic, Inc; "Now I Become Myself", copyright © 1974 by May Sarton, from *Collected Poems 1930–1933* by May Sarton, used by permission of W. W. Norton & Company, Inc; "One Source of Bad Information" from *Morning Poems* by Robert Bly, copyright © 1997 by Robert Bly, reprinted by permission of HarperCollins Publishers; "Gratitude" by Max Kapp copyright © 1977 by Max Kapp, reprinted by permission of Martin Kapp.

When I was an infant, the members of a Unitarian Universalist congregation made promises to me in a typical baby dedication ceremony. They said something like:

Little baby, we will be your springboard as you make your name your own.
We will be your comfort and your inspiration and your joy.
And that's a promise.

They dedicated themselves to me, and they kept their promises. Now, many decades later, it's my turn:

I dedicate this book, with gratitude,
to the people of Unitarian Universalist congregations everywhere,
who offer comfort, inspiration, and joy.

Contents

Foreword

Jane Ranney Rzepka is the first Unitarian Universalist I ever met. I didn't meet her after some service holding a cup of coffee and wearing a name badge—I was fiercely abandoning religion in those days, and kept clear of anything called a church.

Instead, when I met her, she was the twenty-year-old fiancée of my good high school friend Chuck Rzepka, from the Detroit area. I traveled to Ann Arbor, where they were both earning their undergraduate degrees, to meet her. I left that day deeply impressed by her intelligence, clarity, sense of humor, and deft practice of making sure she was never the center of attention.

On that very first day, Chuck mentioned that she had been raised Unitarian Universalist. Not knowing a thing about it, I remember asking her many questions. I was surprised that such a religion existed—it was as if a vast number of people in history had been walking the same path I had in my own little life . . . but I hadn't noticed.

I learned a bit about her Unitarian Universalist heritage that day—some history, some vocabulary. But what moved me more immediately was Jane's honest way of being in the world, and it was clear to me that her life was deeply rooted in her religious upbringing.

Moved by Jane's presence in my life, I forged my own Unitarian Universalist path, joining a church, entering seminary, accepting my first call to a church. But Jane was never far away . . . as the emblematic "non-anxious presence," as a supportive coach, as a trustworthy friend. And, yes, she was a lot more than that too: a scholar who earned a PhD, a supportive spouse to Chuck, a parish minister three times over, an adventuresome world traveler, and the mother of the remarkable Adam and Toby.

When you read this book, it will also be clear that Jane's sense of humor is always near by. Although she and I certainly talk very seriously about our ministerial work, our raft of conversation usually floats on an ocean of laughter.

As you read, you'll see that both her easy laughter, and the jack-in-the-box twinkle in her eye, are woven into the rest of her way of being in the world. This includes a fierce commitment to Unitarian Universalism as a deep and sustaining religious identity. She understands better than most how embracing this identity is. But she is also going to be clear about its centripetal center, the principled sun that holds us all in orbit.

Jane and I have always professed different philosophies about language: she will use *meditation* while I use *prayer* for the same set of words. She prefers to wear "street clothes" when leading worship, whereas I prefer a stole (especially if it matches the flowers!). Yet Jane does not think of me as some "eccentric" Unitarian Universalist, but as someone who roots his practices in our rich, complex heritage just as much as she.

I think Jane's greatest gift is her indefatigable capacity to take the most unexciting events . . . an article in

Newsweek, a routine visit to the dentist, an inane television show with contestants jumping up and down . . . and turn it into a portrait of depth, an evocation of the profound, a signpost of the mysteries, a clear portrait of religious identity. While some might need the turret of the Taj Mahal or the towers at Chartres to pierce the mundane and reveal the holy, Jane usually just opens her eyes and sees what's at hand.

These essays are a literate revelation of Jane's way of living. Here she faithfully affirms what she has been affirming since she was a little girl at the Sunday School in Mentor . . . that life is rich with possibility; that the holy is everywhere if you but notice; that life, despite the reality of misfortune, is no less than amazing; that the ordinary is extraordinary; and that living deliberately with thoughtfulness, kindness, a sense of humor, and a growing aptitude for justice and depth is a gift without peer.

Since I've known and loved her for so long, let me introduce you now. This is Jane Ranney Rzepka.

—Mark Belletini

Introduction

The following pages include amusement parks, Tibetans, Jesus, time capsules, history, justice, zip lines, gods, dinette sets, silence, hosaphones, stars, spirituality, monkeys, free will, matzo, whistlers, forgiveness, Santa, ritual, Pilgrims, worth and dignity, Mad Bacchanalians, connection, bad dancers, affirmation, reason, nose tattoos, liberation, and all around good cheer. Plus a lot more. I can see the question forming in your mind already: "Shouldn't there be some kind of unifying principle?!"

Well, let's see. Were you to write a book report of the sort you wrote in third grade, you might begin by noting that the author is a Unitarian Universalist, through and through. The book, you would say in your report, is organized into three sections, "Straight-Up Unitarian Universalism," "Life," and "Seasons," reminding us of the depth and breadth of seeing life through Unitarian Universalist eyes. That's the unifying principle! And by mentioning the likes of zip lines and hosaphones, it gets right down to brass tacks.

The pieces in this book come from here and there, but almost all of them have their origins in the Unitarian Universalist Church of Reading, Massachusetts, and in the Church of the Larger Fellowship (CLF). Preached as sermons, podcasts, or published in the CLF's *Quest,* these words were written with the faces of real people in my mind's eye, their comments in my ears, their hopes in my spirit. I thank them all for their presence.

But here's the thing. The point. You'll need this for the book report. People need a little something in the religion department. Religion made manifest. We want to be reminded of the glory of the universe, and doing the right thing, and feeling grateful. We want to help out, and be a part of things, large and small. We want to be among those who move toward justice. Toward celebration. Toward love. Things like that.

I hope this helps.

Jane Rzepka
January 1, 2011

Straight-Up Unitarian Universalism

How We Break the Rules

We can wear stripes with plaids now, and socks with open-toed shoes. I know, because I read it in a magazine. "Break the rules," it said. "It's time."

I hate to say it, but rule breaking just might be right up our alley. Maybe it's not the positive tone we try to strike in describing our religion, but I'm going to say right out loud that Unitarian Universalists don't believe in a lot of the rules that our religious neighbors take for granted. Here are nine rules to break regarding religion, just as the magazine did regarding fashion. I'll leave it to you to dream up the tenth.

Religious Rule Number 1:
    You have to sign on to a list of beliefs.
How UUs break the rule:
    We don't have a list of beliefs—no creed; no dogma.

Ultimately, you need to do the work of creating your religious beliefs yourself. You can grow them. You can change them. You can doubt your beliefs, talk about them, try others on for size. Each of us has a unique spirituality, and Unitarian Universalists have a long history of thinking differently as we walk together.

Religious Rule Number 2:
    Obey the hierarchy.

How UUs break the rule:

> We ourselves are the powers that be; there is no hierarchy.

Unitarian Universalism is a democratic religion. The members of the congregation are the boss. You can vote to hold services on Thursday at the zoo instead of Sunday in the regular place; you can criticize the minister—heck, you can fire the minister; you can donate the entire congregational budget to . . . well, the mind boggles. Lay people are powerful, and they're where the buck stops.

Religious Rule Number 3:

> You must perform the rituals.

How UUs break the rule:

> We have no prescribed rituals.

Some Unitarian Universalists appreciate ritual, some do not. It's as simple as that. You decide. If you want to welcome your baby into the world with a service, that's great. If you always take a moment for gratitude before eating, or begin each day with music, a poem, or tea and the *Times*, you may feel the better for it. If a regular practice enlivens you and urges you toward the good, you have found your ritual.

Religious Rule Number 4:

> You have to believe in God to be religious.

How UUs break the rule:

    No, you don't.

We all know people who think that a person cannot be religious—or even behave—without believing in a god or gods. Unitarian Universalists are free to live their experience of both heart and mind, welcoming the atheists, humanists, agnostics, and those beyond categorizing among us, as well as those who find meaning in a personal or impersonal god.

Religious Rule Number 5:

    Your religious beliefs should be based on faith.

How UUs break the rule:

    Our religious beliefs are based on reason and
    experience. Faith is optional.

If you're inclined toward the empirical and experiential, Unitarian Universalism will work fine for you. If faith provides you with a spiritual strategy, and it doesn't contradict what we know to be true, then faith is yours. There's room for us all.

Religious Rule Number 6:

    Some objects, spaces, and events are inherently
    sacred.

How UUs break the rule:

    Nothing—or everything—is inherently sacred.

Surely we feel grateful, respectful, appreciative, even wowed at times, but we aren't accustomed by history or tradition to set spaces, objects, or events apart from our ordinary lives. We'd rather they were close at hand.

Religious Rule Number 7:
    Heresy is bad.
How UUs break the rule:
    Heresy can be heroic.

Throughout our history, we have often identified with theological heresies. Are human beings depraved at birth? Unitarian Universalists say no. Are events predetermined? We say no. Do people go to hell? No. Is Jesus God? Again, no. Are scriptures infallible? We say no.

I have heard that when the late Dana McLean Greeley, then president of the Unitarian Universalist Association, met with Pope John XXIII at the Vatican II Council, the Pope said, with a twinkle in his eye, "You made a religion of all our heresies." The Pope was right.

Religious Rule Number 8:
    Religion is not fun.
How UUs break the rule:
    Religion runs the gamut, and for us the gamut includes fundamental joy, bemusement, and the frequent hearty laugh.

We live a positive religion that embraces what is good in the world, including simple pleasures that remind us how wonderful it can be to be alive. We find no particular merit in the stuffy. To chuckle over a good-natured story during a memorial service, to emerge from meditation with a smile, to erupt with happiness at news of a new baby, to glory in the fun of a job well done—it's all religious.

Religious Rule Number 9:
    Religion is stifling.
How UUs break the rule:
    Well, we rock.

If I do say so myself. In our diversity, we embrace more diversity still. We stand for freedom. We nourish one another. We look forward to scientific breakthroughs; creative social justice initiatives; new ways of peace, both inner and outer; and the adventures and styles and contributions of those who are younger. We try, anyway. Revelation is not sealed.

I'm Not Just Saying This

"I'm not just saying this because I'm your mother. Now listen, and believe me, you are the prettiest, nicest girl in the entire school, not to mention the brightest, and if you don't believe me just go look in the mirror. I happen to know that there are dozens of young men who would give their eye teeth to go out with a wonderful girl like you. Boys are shy, too, you know. Don't you worry, someday your ship will come in."

Actually, that little speech? That's the full title of this sermon.

We could all use that kind of speech from somebody who grabs us by the lapels in the morning, looks us square in the eye, and says, "Listen. You are wonderful. You have what it takes. We all like *what* you are and *who* you are. You do a good job at life. We care about you; we love you. Count on that. Don't ever doubt that." And then you go off and begin your day.

Healthy little kids know they're hot stuff. Little kids strut. Little kids say what they think. When you tell José he looks terrific in his new shoes, he'll say, "I know." What happens to that? How do we lose that certainty that we look terrific in our new shoes?

Well, we get battered about. Some big kid says that the new shoes are for babies. Grandma treats the new shoes as "just shoes." José loses sight of the bouncy, resilient child he is and "becomes" his shoes. That's the short answer: we lose sight of the good, solid citizen inside, the divinity within, and adopt what we think we heard from the outside world as a comment on our very core as a human being.

In a Sunday service some years back, a colleague, Forrest Church, asked people in the pews to look at a person sitting next to them or in front of them or behind them. He said, "I'll make a bet with you. I bet that at least one of your neighbors in the pews looks as if he or she knows something that you don't know. Or looks like they have their act together. And I'll bet something else. I'll bet that when they were looking at you, they were thinking the same thing."

Not that most of us are on the brink of psychological disaster. We're just inclined to imagine that the people around us have smoother lives—they're less lonely, or more in control of their anger. They're neater, or surer, their children don't talk back, they have more close friends, fewer money worries, more job satisfaction, a better sex life. There's a lot of looking around, a lot of not feeling so very good inside.

It's self-esteem that can go to bat for us. Self-esteem is our reputation with ourselves, how we hold ourselves in our own estimation. The poet Derek Walcott writes,

The time will come
when, with elation
you will greet yourself arriving
at your own door, in your own mirror
and each will smile at the other's welcome . . .

That's good self-esteem. It's a feeling, not a score card. It doesn't matter whether or not you are the best bowler on the team, or the worst; the best salesperson in the company or the worst; fat or thin; indebted or rolling in dough. It is psycho-epistemological—at the very root of your being—what you think you're like, not what you do.

At about the time we begin to talk about aspects of life so basic, as basic as self-esteem, we find that we're talking about religion. What are we like? What is human nature? Do we start off corrupt at birth, or do we come equipped with an essential goodness inside? Is there a power that makes us what we are? Are we sheep waiting to be led, or are we more or less in charge of the direction of our lives?

These questions are not merely angels-on-the-head-of-a-pin theological; they directly affect the way we feel about ourselves. Unitarian Universalists are fortunate in this regard, because our religious tradition has always gone hand-in-hand with the fostering of self-worth. We have battled the concept of original sin for two hundred years.

Imagine a mindset in which you are at your very core depraved and sinful, before you even get started. Imagine—and I know some of you were raised this way and don't have to imagine—the weight and pain of trying to live a healthy and satisfying life knowing always how lowly you are. The Calvinist system works for lots of people and I appreciate that, but for me its appeal is nearly impossible to comprehend.

From the Unitarian side of our history, we have, in the mid-1700s, leading Boston ministers Jonathan Mayhew and Charles Chauncy emphasizing the good in human nature—radically stating that our natural powers can be cultivated and improved until we attain an actual likeness to God. From the Universalist side, we inherit the words popularly attributed to John Murray: "You possess a small light . . . uncover it, let it shine, use it in order to bring more light and understanding to the hearts and minds of men and women. Give them not hell, but hope and courage."

Later, of course, we have Ralph Waldo Emerson claiming that within us is "the soul of the whole; the wise silence; the universal beauty. . . . When it breaks through our intellect, it is genius; when it breathes through our will, it is virtue; when it flows through our affections, it is love." If any of this theology sinks into us or our children (and I believe it does), our self-esteem is wonderfully supported. We mustn't take this spiritual blessing for granted.

OK. Healthy self-esteem is something we believe in. But believing in it isn't enough—we have to figure out how to get it! And just when we're busy figuring out how to get it, we remember that Unitarian Universalism tells us we already have it! Our theological ancestors pointed out that actually, there's nothing we have to do—we simply "possess a small light" that we need only "uncover" and "let shine."

My own favorite image is of a new baby, about three months old. A three-month-old baby is a pretty pure form of life, and when you hold that baby and look into its eyes, you smile. You just do. The baby hasn't come home with a good report card, the baby isn't the author of a best-selling screenplay, the baby doesn't have a fancy new hair-do, the baby—just by virtue of being alive—is good enough to be smiled at. So are we all.

But it doesn't always feel that way.

I performed a wedding once and had a little trouble with the marriage license: it blew away. It just sailed into the heavens on that windy wedding day, and was never seen again.

So I went to Boston City Hall. I had my ordination certificate along, and the wedding ceremony, the couple's check, our parish register, church letterhead, and my driver's license. But the woman said, "No dice. I have to see the church records." It did no good to point out that these *were* the church records—she wasn't budging. Neither of us, it turned out, could imagine exactly what kind of "church records" would suffice.

After a couple of hours of this, I, too, began to doubt that I'd ever performed the wedding, become a minister, or been born and given a name.

As an adolescent, when I sometimes doubted my existence or my place in the universe, I turned to the existentialists, if only to confirm the legitimacy of the doubt. But the actual healing always came from the love, or even the nonchalant acceptance, of people around me. We must remember to do that for each other, even when we're stuck behind the marriage license window at City Hall.

The expert on this, of course, was the TV personality Mister Rogers, Fred Rogers. Frankly, I never took to Fred. He was just so sappy, and, to tell you the truth, I get a little queasy when I even think of the tune, "It's a Beautiful Day in the Neighborhood." But when it comes to self-esteem, Mister Rogers was a pro. I hesitate to mention the tunes he sang for fear that those old enough to remember will burst into song right there on the bus or at the hair dresser or wherever you're reading this, but he wrote pieces like "Everybody's Fancy": "Some are fancy on the outside, some are fancy on the inside. Everybody's fancy. Everybody's fine." Or, "It's such a good feeling to know you're alive," or "You can never go down, can never go down, can never go down the drain."

We don't, most of us, have Mister Rogers to remind us every day that we can't go down the drain and we're plenty fancy just the way we are. But we do have each other. It doesn't take much.

This is what we can do: We can accept and affirm one another.

We don't have to approve of our neighbors' tax forms or lawn care or voting record to approve of their humanness. We don't have to be dazzled by our spouse's or roommate's performance as a washer of clothes or cars to offer an extra affectionate word or gesture. We need not be at all impressed with the state of our children's room to open our arms to them. There's a cartoon that says, and it's true, "By accepting you as you are, I do not necessarily abandon all hope of your improving."

Inside you know you're terrific in your new shoes. You know, and I'm not just saying this because I'm your mother, you know, that you're the prettiest, nicest girl in the entire class. And when you forget all that, when you've lost sight of how holy you are, when you've lost track of the miracle that you are, when you don't feel at all to be the wondrous human being that you are, somebody will remind you because you once reminded them. And then,

The time will come
when, with elation
you will greet yourself arriving
at you own door, in your own mirror
and each will smile at the other's welcome . . .

The Latest on Jesus

One of the religion writers at *Newsweek* magazine is panic stricken. He has been investigating the latest scholarship about Jesus, and he can't believe his ears. He's discovered that the experts believe that the real Jesus was no more the child of God than anyone else. They tell him that Jesus was a Jewish peasant, and probably illiterate. A compelling itinerant preacher and social revolutionary, Jesus challenged Roman rulers and Jewish leaders. He may have been peaceful, but he was clearly outspoken.

How hard it must have been for the *Newsweek* journalist, Mr. Russell Watson, to hear that Jesus performed no miracles; called for an egalitarian Kingdom of God which would manifest not in Heaven, but in the here and now; and wanted people to experience God directly, unimpeded by hierarchy of temple or state. The scholars would have told Watson that the authorities executed Jesus rather routinely after he caused a disturbance in Jerusalem during Passover, that Jesus did not physically rise from the dead, and that his body was probably buried in a shallow grave.

The *Newsweek* journalist is utterly bewildered by this description of Jesus: incredulous, horror-struck. He concludes, "If that's who Jesus was, then every important article of the traditional Christian faith goes out the window —no virgin birth, no divine nature and, most devastating of all, no Resurrection. This is a portrait of a Jesus no one ever encountered in Sunday school."

So I'm reading along there in *Newsweek* magazine, and I've got to tell you, I get a little agitated myself. I'm reading along . . . "no virgin birth," "no miracles," "no Judgment Day," "no church hierarchy," "no divine nature," "no bodily resurrection"—unlike Mr. Watson, I'm doing fine so far. The article goes on, Jesus was a "spell-binding preacher," a "peaceful" reformer, "accepting" and "loving," who "lived on in the hearts of followers." In fact I'm doing great with all this until I hit the very last sentence where he says, "This is a portrait of a Jesus no one ever encountered in Sunday school."

Excuse me. I did. That's exactly the Jesus I encountered in Sunday school. Right down the line. We learned all about that Jesus when I was a Unitarian child, just as most Unitarian Universalist children do now: Jesus the teacher, Jesus the reformer, Jesus the source of inspiration —as our old Unitarian Sunday school textbook put it in its title, *Jesus, the Carpenter's Son.* Copyrighted in 1945, the book, written by Sophia Fahs—one of our greatest religious educators—was used for years and years. It paints exactly the portrait of Jesus that *Newsweek* claims "no one ever encountered in Sunday school."

Sophia Fahs is a pretty big deal for liberal religion, not so much for the down-to-earth picture of Jesus she taught, but for her methodology and her respectful attitude toward children. Listen to what she says to our children about Jesus in 1945: "Was Jesus real or was he just a story person? When he was a baby did he know that he was different from all other babies? Could Jesus do anything he wanted to do? Did he die because he wanted to die, or couldn't he help being killed? Why do some people say he is 'the Son of God'? Does God have only one son? These are questions some boys and girls have asked. They have felt confused."

She goes on to encourage children to put their ideas and questions about Jesus into words, to accept only what makes sense to them about Jesus and the Bible, and to "take responsibility for their own thoughts." "You need to be prepared to question [the stories]. Keep your minds awake. Ask yourselves: Could this have happened? Read for yourselves the verses in the gospel records. Use your own imaginations. Bring [Jesus] to life, as it were, in your imagination, so that you will be emotionally stirred as you surely would have been had you actually seen and heard him."

Sophia Fahs would be happy to know that she is not alone in approaching the question of Jesus in this spirit; increasingly in mainline Christian denominations, scholars do too.

It's a funny thing about scholarship. I always thought that you take a subject, Jesus in this case, you learn more and more, and after years of research, ta-da, you have a fairly complete picture—at least you know a whole lot more about him than when you began. But when studying Jesus, the opposite is true. As Robert Funk points out in his *Honest to Jesus*, you think you know the general story of Jesus to begin with, but the more you investigate, the more you discover that a lot of what you thought you

17

knew isn't true, and that the amount of information we can really document about Jesus' life gets smaller and smaller as we learn more. As your body of knowledge increases, you find more and more discrepancies between the Jesus portrayed in Bible stories and the actual historical Jesus.

Here's what happens. You read the four Gospels, Matthew, Mark, Luke, and John, and you notice that they include not one unified account of Jesus' life but four different interpretations—that's how John Dominic Crossan describes the process in *Jesus: A Revolutionary Biography*. Then you read further accounts in other Gospels that have been recently discerned as sources, such as the so-called Q Gospel, and you read those Gospels that have been found that were not included in the Bible, The Gospel of Thomas, for example, found in Upper Egypt in 1945. Then you study cross-cultural anthropology, and then Greco-Roman and Jewish history at the time of Jesus. And instead of lots of new information with which to bolster the stories of the typical picture of Jesus, you are left with a short list of information—the "no-frills Jesus," as it was described in the *Atlantic* some years back.

To wit: most critical scholars agree that Jesus' hometown was Nazareth, and he was probably born there as well, contrary to later legends that assign his birth to Bethlehem to satisfy an ancient prophecy. His mother's name was Mary. Jesus had four brothers, and he may also have had some sisters.

His native tongue was Aramaic. We don't know whether Jesus could read and write. We don't know whether or not he knew Hebrew. There is now evidence that suggests he may have been bilingual; Greek was probably his second language, learned from the pagan environment that surrounded him in Galilee. We do not know how long his public career lasted, but the narrative Gospels imply a relatively short period, from one to three years.

In *Honest to Jesus*, Funk says that Jesus had

> no permanent address, no bed to sleep in, and no respect on his home turf. He did not ask disciples to convert the world and establish a church. Unlike John the Baptist, he did not believe the world was going to end immediately, he did not even call on people to repent, and he did not practice baptism. He may have eaten a last meal with the inner circle of his followers, but he did not initiate what we know as the Eucharist.

When I read along in this vein, I have this little nagging voice in the back of my mind asking, "Yes, this Jesus scholarship is fun, but is it important? Does it really matter?" As one generous scholar, Marcus Borg, notes, "There are millions of people for whom the older image of Jesus still works. And they have absolutely no need to pay any attention to us."

Why would it matter that the real Jesus didn't baptize, if baptism offers comfort or renewal to modern day folks? Who cares if the resurrection was a fabrication born of grief, political necessity, or blind faith, if it serves a hopeful function in society today? Why rain on the parade of people who believe Jesus looked like them and spoke English (the King James Version in fact), and smelled good, and didn't drink, and advocated traditional American upscale family life in the suburbs?

The daily newspaper gave me an answer to my questions. There was a news story a while back about a play in New Jersey, the Passion Play about Jesus' last days, where, for the first time in the theater's 82-year run, a black man had been cast as Jesus.

Five tour groups canceled their reservations. Others wanted to reschedule for performances when a white actor played Jesus. After a couple of vague death threats were phoned into the theater, two church schools canceled out of fear for the safety of their students.

This story of racism is horrifying—that goes without saying. But it is born, in part, of ignorance. Why in the world do potential members of the audience think that Jesus, a resident of the Middle East, would look like white people in New Jersey?!

Knowledge, learning, the study of the historical Jesus would have helped here. Knowing the facts of Jesus' life would have stopped the appropriation of Jesus by those who use him to promote values thoroughly at odds with what he really stood for.

One of the recent scholarly depictions of Jesus is that he was a social deviant of the sort we'd do well to emulate, who fully accepted his fellow human beings, no matter how disreputable or marginal they seemed in the eyes of society. We are acquiring a deeper awareness that Jesus "kept an open table," that is to say, again according to Funk, that "he ate promiscuously with sinners, toll collectors, prostitutes, lepers, and other social misfits and quarantined people." He robbed humankind of all "protections and privileges, entitlements and ethnicities that segregate human beings into categories."

Peter Gomes, who wrote *The Good Book*, goes a little further when he says that inclusion can legitimately be claimed "by the poor, persons of color, gays, lesbians and transgender people, women, and all persons beyond the conventional definitions of Western civilization." When we study the record, when we learn what there is to learn about the historical Jesus, and model ourselves after what's best in his teachings, every Christian, and any of us here who choose to follow the example of Jesus, will see the value of an open table.

Studying the historical Jesus is not only academically interesting, but also socially and religiously responsible for all of us who live in Western culture. When a neighbor claims that the Jesus cast in the Passion play needs to be white, we can state our case. And when Jesus is held up as a spokesperson for reactionary so-called "family values," or for the exclusion of non-Christians, or gay people, or people of color, or any group at all, we'll know to shout in protest; we'll fight for that open table.

In the words of Robert Funk, "The Jesus of that alternative world encourages me to celebrate life, to suck the marrow out of existence, to explore, and probe, and experiment, to venture into uncharted seas. . . . He does not set limits on my curiosity, on my drive to challenge every axiom. That same Jesus prompts me to give myself to tasks that exceed, even contradict, my own self-interest. I am not infrequently startled at the tasks I find myself willing to undertake."

Come to think of it, I learned all that in Sunday school.

Here it is September, that traditional "church shopping" time of the year. Of course, we're always delighted when questions lead newcomers to Unitarian Universalism.

Whether you come to a Unitarian Universalist church by means of the Web, a podcast, a copy of a sermon, an online quiz, the front door of a congregation, or at the kind invitation of a friend, your questions about Unitarian Universalism often include something about god.

What is god in the context of the Unitarian Universalist religion? Of course, many don't find the word *god*, or even the concept, helpful at all, but many do. And many more are intrigued by what one might call "the changing face of god," where god becomes a goddess, or a cosmos that's generally friendly, or a free-floating inclination toward the good, or an omnipresence that helps us to behave. Some look for an image of god that promotes healing, or wholeness, or inner calm, or acceptance, or guidance. Others are drawn to images or conceptions from traditional religions—Jewish, maybe, or Pagan, Muslim, or Christian. Unitarian Universalists have Sunday school curricula that encourage our children to explore all kinds of ideas of god, including no god at all.

Some questioners step back and wonder why so many images of god appear in human form. The short answer seems to be that that's what people do. Peter Berger's *Sacred Canopy* tells us that human beings externalize, that it's an anthropological necessity. In *The History of God*, Karen Armstrong claims that throughout the ages, people have conceptualized the gods that worked for them in their own time and in their own place: that each generation creates its own god.

We look back and remember that the Romans held Caesar to be a god, and the Egyptian pharaohs became gods, as did the Greek Dionysus, and Jesus. Western history in particular has a habit of apotheosizing people, turning them into gods. They become not just superheroes, but supernatural heroes. Or at least that's how the history appears to many of us living in the twenty-first century.

A colleague, Laura Cavicchio, once did some research about the goddess Anath, popular about the time that the god of the Hebrew Scriptures was developing. Anath is an anthropomorphic goddess—she looks like us—but she's a super-powerful warrior goddess: "She killed the people of the coast / she annihilated the men of the east. . . . / She plunged knee-deep into the soldiers' blood, up to her thighs in the warriors' gore." Different people, different cultures, need different concepts of the divine at different times and places, depending on their circumstances.

So of course there are thousands and thousands of gods out there. All of us sit in our own cultures looking out at the gods, and we see what *we* see, not what believers see. Some gods seem completely abstract to me, but their manifestations look concrete. The Hindu supreme being Ishvara, for example, manifests as the physical

Vishnu and Shiva. Buddhism seems to have the same sort of arrangement to this outsider. Buddhism is not based on a god at all, but still you wind up with a panoply of popular gods and demons derived and assimilated from indigenous folk religions.

Meanwhile, the Jewish god looks to me to be a personal god, yet is never described or given a visual image, nor, in the strict sense, is god's name ever to be spoken. Somehow, though this god has no physicality, we imagine this god to be male. This male image was inherited by both Christianity and Islam.

We can look back and forth through time and over and around the world, and Karen Armstrong's observation seems to be true: if we do need gods, we create the gods we need.

What gods, if any, does a religious liberal look for?

Of course that question is yours to answer. Although atheism, agnosticism, and humanism are welcome and particularly popular, among Unitarian Universalists some gods are common.

God may be a spirit that offers a feeling of safety and advocacy close at hand, a feeling of belonging wherever you are. A warmth, a confidence, an acceptance.

Others experience a god that provides strength and encouragement, especially in the face of life's challenges. A god that understands how difficult their situation is and how hard they are trying, as only a god can.

Still others experience a cosmic kind of god that inclines some things to happen and others not to, or balances the good in the universe with the not-so-good, or tips the balance toward the positive.

Some among us feel a life-force in the world, an energy, a liveliness, a connection that is not so much personal but universal.

No two Unitarian Universalist theists conceptualize their gods in exactly the same way—at least that's my guess. But when people in our fold want a god in their lives, they are inclined to welcome a face of god that gives them strength for the good, with meaning and love.

Informed by religions of the world and our own unique needs and experiences, a number of options are out there for those who are interested. That, in my view, is what a church shopper needs to know about Unitarian Universalism and god.

To Pray or Not to Pray

Here's how it looks to me: something in our hearts says, "Help me, I need somebody to lean on, to depend on, or to guide me, or rescue me," or "Please, it's the beginning of May, let spring come to New England." Or "Let my fortunes turn, I've suffered enough," or "I'll do anything, just make my baby get well." The root word for prayer is from the Latin, *precarius*, "obtained by begging." Don't you know that feeling? That's just how it seems to work with human beings.

All of which puts a lot of Unitarian Universalists in something of an awkward situation. And the situation is this: Many of us, not all of us of course, but a lot of us, don't find traditional forms of prayer of particular use. According to an extensive article in *Newsweek* some time back, "Prayer presupposes a God who can be addressed." And that presupposition can be a problem for those Unitarian Universalists who don't posit a god at all, or who don't posit a god who has ears, either literally or metaphorically.

Rev. Max Coots once explained,

Until recently, as history goes, almost everyone assumed that God, by whatever name and in whatever form, was the omnipotent puppeteer pulling the strings that controlled everything from amoebae to empires, from ants to conquering armies, from the movement of the stars to the state of your digestion.

But, after 50,000 years of such unquestioned divine attention, people began to realize that the earth was not the center of the universe; that stars were not tiny, friendly night lights lovingly hung for us; that space stretched out beyond imagination; that spring and summer came whether or not we praised the sun; that it was microscopic organisms, unaware of our personal piety, that brought disease; and that death came to believer and unbeliever alike here on the earth, spinning in its tiny orbit around its little star in one corner of one galaxy in a sea of galaxies in space.

While we may feel the basic urge to petition for our greatest personal needs, we can't quite believe in that puppeteer in the sky who would pull just the strings we need. While we experience the universal tendency to praise what seems wondrous around us, while we want to say with E. E. Cummings, "i thank you god for most this amazing day," it is the rare Unitarian Universalist who can imagine an anthropomorphic addressee to whom our appreciation should be sent. While we know we would appreciate some guidance now and then, we have trouble postulating a divine twenty-four-hour texting service. And while we may ache for soothing, healing powers, we don't want to think that a god is up there granting some prayers, and denying others just as worthy.

Unitarian Universalists have a few strategies about prayer that deal with this theological quandary. Let's call it two strategies, to simplify. They both work great, they both have roots within our Unitarian Universalist history, and they both invite spiritual maturity.

Here's the first: Some UUs use the word *prayer* as an expression of their personal spiritual life. Typically, they broaden the definition of prayer to encompass a wide variety of spiritual practices and centering activities. And so if they are focused on the first snowdrops of the season, they may be praying; or if they are soaking in the tub, they may be praying; or if they are participating in the walk for hunger, they may be praying; or if they are tucking their two-year-old in at night, they may be praying. To pray they look deep inside, they talk to a friend, they walk, they drive, they sing, they blog, they meditate or contemplate, they prune the trees, they touch their toes, they sit together in church.

Rev. Mark Belletini writes,

So prayer can be words, silence, song, or as Paul of Tarsus says, "a sigh." Prayer can be one prophet breaking the bread of affliction with tears in his eyes and another breaking a clay pot with eyes ablaze. Whatever cuts through our defensiveness, whether it's disguised as a sense of worthlessness or a sense of hubris, is a great prayer. Crafted or spontaneous, elegant or halted with sobs, sung to God, danced to Love Most Deep or simply uttered into the thin air, prayer . . . is the life-breath of . . . worship.

Yes. We may broaden the definition of prayer, until, in the extreme form, we may even say, along with the Unitarian Susan B. Anthony, "I pray every single second of my life; not on my knees but with my work."

But for many Unitarian Universalists, broadening the definition of prayer, or using the word at all, makes no sense. And so the second strategy is this: these UUs don't pray—they strive to feel awake to life, embrace the grandeur of living on this planet, explore those aspects of life that ground them, connect to people and places and the cosmos in general, contribute to the healthy future of neighbors the world over, note beauty in a variety of forms, and value the trajectory toward health and well-being. That kind of thing. They don't pray.

Just like the group that does pray, this group focuses on the same first snowdrops of the season, soaks in tubs, participates in the walk for hunger, tucks the two-year-old in at night, looks deep inside, talks to friends, walks, drives, sings, blogs, meditates or contemplates, prunes the trees, touches their toes, sits together in church. But let me be clear: these UUs are not praying, and there is no reason in the world to impose the language of prayer on them. You ask a conventional Roman Catholic, or a Lutheran, or a Southern Baptist, not to mention a Muslim or a Jew—you ask any of them if Unitarian Universalists pray, and most of them will tell you that this "Spirit of Life" business, this meditation and spiritual practice business, absolutely does not cut it as prayer.

The truth is, our history with respect to prayer is different. In the mid-eighteen hundreds, Samuel Longfellow and Henry Longfellow, raised in the First Parish in Portland, Maine, and a generation later, Rev. Frederick Hosmer, began to write hymns that spoke of nature and social concern instead of the traditional God and prayer. Unitarian Universalists still sing those hymns: "O Life that Maketh All Things New," "God of the Earth, the Sky, the Sea," and "Lo, the Earth is Ris'n Again," often sung on Easter. All of those are by Samuel Longfellow, a Unitarian minister. Henry, his brother, wrote "All Are Architects of Fate," number 288 in our hymn book, *Singing the Living Tradition*. Hosmer wrote "Forward Through the Ages," and he wrote "Lo, the Day of Days Is Here" and "O Day of Light and Gladness," two more often sung on Easter. Thomas Starr King, our notable minister in San Francisco during that time, said, "We find God in nature. We find God in Mt. Shasta as in Mt. Hermon, and do not fear to say so on Sunday." Already, even then, we began to sound like contemporary Unitarian Universalists.

Personally, I come out of the Midwestern tradition of Unitarianism, and my great-grandparents' minister said in a sermon about prayer, "I have frankly and completely given it up. . . . I believe we must give it up." Even now, my own theological language reflects my Midwestern Unitarian heritage, and I do not pray.

But what language you use is not so important, really. What is important is this: we are people. And people sometimes feel lonely or afraid or overwhelmed or a little uncertain. We are people. And people sometimes feel consumed by the wonder of it all, the majesty of creation, the joy and good fortune of living in this world. We are people. And people sometimes feel they need a healing touch, a sturdy companion, a safe harbor, an accepting, loving friend, always there. That's what's important. Go ahead. Call it prayer if you want to. Or call it your religion. You are a Unitarian Universalist. You have a choice.

Our Slippery Spirituality

If there's a slipperier yet more persistent topic than Unitarian Universalist spirituality, I don't know what it is. I can pretty much assure you that when you hear the word in conversation, unless you ask, you don't know precisely what it means—and maybe not even then. At the same time, many are tired of talking about what spirituality means—it seems like a waste of time, when vocabulary really isn't the point.

Yet when it comes to Unitarian Universalist spirituality, questions come forth relentlessly. Does spirituality have to involve something greater than yourself? Can you come by it naturally, or do you have to work at it? Is a spiritual person different from a person who is simply grounded, kind, generous, and reflective? Do you even have to use the word?

To be sure, one can find folks among us who will declare quite definitively what spirituality is and how to get some. But as a UU minister, I'm not here to hem you in. Let me just say that I have noticed some people who seem spiritual to everyone around them. They just do. These everyday spiritual people live the kind of spirituality we all wish we had. Are they all old and wise? No. Do they all have spiritual disciplines? No. Are they all selfless in the face of need? No. Do they all believe in God? No. They are young musicians and tow truck drivers and retired umpires. They memorize poetry, snorkel, engage rigorously with what needs doing, practice Yoga, or read the Bible. They are the life of the party or book worms. They tend to the dying, trim their neighbors' hedges, lobby for change, or donate a kidney. They take time for quiet every morning, or they chug a cup of coffee and out the door they go. The template is hard to discern, and yet we call them spiritual. We see it, we know it.

What do they have in common? You'll come up with your own list, but it seems to me, first, that spiritual people seem anchored, grounded.

Metaphor and symbol often help. Maybe early on they practiced connecting and drawing strength from lyrics in their big sister's music collection, or the sapling growing in the face of adversity behind the McDonald's, reading *Anne of Green Gables,* or skipping stones. They continued to grow and learn to find the noble, healthy symbols—the ones they'd call sacred. The images and experiences began to sink in: the stories, the music, the physicality, the connections, until something good and solid took form inside. And when they pause, this inner life is available to sustain, hold, inspire, and offer meaning to them.

What else do spiritual people have in common? I'd say they have perspective. They understand the difference between car trouble and war casualties, between a pimple on prom night and, say, global warming.

Isn't that what people mean when they tell us to "get a grip"? They want us to take a deep breath, and get in touch with what really matters. To get out of ourselves a little and show some gratitude for what's going right. Spiritual people aren't so quick to get ruffled, or irritated, or angry—unless there's a principle at stake. A religious value. Then they take action. People say they "have it together."

What else? Love. Again, we get to practice. From teddy bears to first bikes to crushes on teachers to passions for the kid who has the locker next to ours, love gets a workout. But in the spiritual people we see around us, love demonstrates a pervasive quality.

They get along fine with almost everybody—it feels good to be in their presence. They're good eggs. They love life enough for belly laughs. They actively love the human family, and life on the planet, and their love seems to radiate—at least a little—as far as imagination goes.

That's what I notice about spiritual people for starters: they are grounded, they have perspective, and they love. Spirituality isn't ever a done deal though, it's always a process—no one is ever fully spiritually mature.

Some of us long for a step-by-step process, a one-size-fits-all program for spiritual formation. So far, human history hasn't developed that product. But we know that choices range from back-packing to helping out in the aftermath of deadly storms to therapy to singing country western songs from the bottom of your heart. Silent retreats. Bedtime stories. Wind in your hair. Good deeds every day. Gratitude. Praying. Stars above the parking lot. If you want to develop your spirituality, keep your program going.

Retired UU minister Charles Wilson once wrote,

Clearly, to be a spiritual being is to be more than oneself, not at rest but in motion, on one's way to a fuller and deeper self. . . . Why do it? To learn how to handle dynamite.

It's as good a time as any to go deeper into a personal religious life. To find what it is that works for you, drawing you toward wholeness.

If You Are There, I Am Glad

"There are creatures in the deep caves of Mercury." That's how a passage by Kurt Vonnegut begins in *The Sirens of Titan*. So we are imagining that on the planet Mercury "the creatures in the caves look very much like small and spineless kites. They are diamond-shaped, a foot high and eight inches wide when fully mature," and "they have no more thickness than the skin of a toy balloon." They cling to the walls of their caves, for they are nourished by vibrations.

I'm not much of a science fiction fan, but here's the part that captures my attention: By means of the vibrations of the caves' walls, creatures on Mercury have weak powers of telepathy as they live there in the caves, clinging. The first message is an automatic response to the second, and the second is an automatic response to the first.

Here's the first message: "Here I am, here I am, here I am."

The response? "So glad you are, so glad you are, so glad you are."

The creatures are called harmoniums.

Unitarian Universalists talk a lot about the inherent worth and dignity of each person. Worth and dignity. Rolls right off the tongue. It amounts to, "If you are there, I am glad"—or at least respectful.

Occasionally we may ask ourselves, "Is it really true? Is my religion asking me to be a harmonium?" Aren't there people who on the face of it seem wholly undignified and unworthy, exceptions to the dignity and worth rule? Hitler and evil come quickly to mind, and those who have done us harm—or who have harmed the world or the innocents or the people we love. Maybe the UU notion that every person deserves dignity and worth is pushing it. I've certainly heard the case made.

I'll tell you where I am on this. Day to day, I try to go with the harmoniums. In a theological discussion I might make a concession or two, but mostly I believe in the "Here I am/So glad you are" approach.

I have a mental image of a huge collage made up of pictures of hands. Little tiny hands, gnarled hands, hands with tattoos on them or rings, hands showing spots or scars, trembling hands, perfectly smooth hands, big strong hands, delicate hands, even metaphorical hands. Hands we love, mysterious hands, firm hand-shaking hands, good hands to hold.

To qualify for inclusion in the collage, your hands would have no tests to pass, no theological criteria to fulfill or mandatory number of good works in their history. No one would ask if your hands voted as political liberals or conservatives, how much they dropped into the coffers of the local congregation, or whom they loved or how. Your hand would be worthy of our display because it is your hand. Every hand a worthy hand; our theology made flesh.

Perhaps because it appears as a responsive reading in our hymn book, *Singing the Living Tradition*, a number of Unitarian Universalists can more or less recite Mary Oliver's poem "Wild Geese."

You do not have to be good.
You do not have to walk on your knees
for a hundred miles through the desert, repenting.
You only have to let the soft animal of your body
    love what it loves.
Tell me about despair, yours, and I will tell you mine.
Meanwhile the world goes on.
Meanwhile the sun and the clear pebbles of the rain
are moving across the landscapes,
over the prairies and the deep trees,
the mountains and the rivers.
Meanwhile the wild geese, high in the clean blue air,
are heading home again.
Whoever you are, no matter how lonely,
the world offers itself to your imagination,
calls to you like the wild geese, harsh and exciting—
over and over announcing your place
in the family of things.

That's our general theological position as Unitarian Universalists. Each of us has a place in the family of things. We know that there are people who have been startlingly rude or breathtakingly gracious. People who thwart all progress and people who make the ride easy, people who say what they feel and people who keep us all guessing, people who let us down and people who stun us with their accomplishments. Consistent people, unpredictable people. Givers. Takers. People who lose it, people who keep it together. Smilers, frowners. But we move forward assuming that somewhere inside each of those people is a person of dignity and worth.

It is February, so I wanted to write about love. Here's what I know about one way of loving: a reverberating, harmonious perpetual Valentine's Day. Somebody out there sends the signal: "Here I am, here I am, here I am." The response? "So glad you are, so glad you are, so glad you are."

Science, Spirituality, Religion and All That

The problem with talking about religion and science is that there is no problem. We're Unitarian Universalists. We're pro-religion, and we're pro-science. That's been true for generations. Nothing's changed since 1947 when Unitarian minister A. Powell Davies wrote, "To those who are accustomed to the liberal viewpoint in religion, it may seem surprising that anyone should wish to discuss the rather elementary question as to whether science and religion can get together. In liberal churches, it has been taken for granted for almost a generation that nothing substantial has ever kept them apart."

But the topic persists, even today. "Creation science." "Intelligent design." Sometimes it seems as though science and religion really do need to duke it out. Take the subject of smallpox, now eliminated from the planet. In the 1960s, science believed it could vaccinate against smallpox; indeed, it knew that it could eradicate smallpox. But religion believed in the local smallpox gods. In India it was the goddess Shitala; in Africa it was the god Shapona. Smallpox vaccinations would elicit the wrath of the smallpox gods, causing unbridled outbreaks; indeed, religion knew this to be true. And there you have the problem—a direct conflict between science and religion.

Historically, who loses in the conflict between traditional religion and science? Religion. Does anyone believe in the Greek gods anymore, or the Roman pantheon?

Increasingly, across the globe populations abandon rain dances to elicit precipitation, exorcisms in the face of mental illness, sacrifices of animals to insure the harvest. Religion loses—slowly, surely.

Yet whenever science wins, Unitarian Universalism somehow wins as well. We are, in a word, an oddball religion—not the only one, but still unusual—a religion prone to the search for a truth that includes scientific truth, and not at all inclined toward adherence to a doctrine frozen in time. When science scores a point, so do we.

Science discovers new fossils of primitive humans? We think that's amazing. Possible organisms on Mars? Cool. Let's do more research. Evolution embraces the impact of random cataclysmic events. Wow!

You say you want to feel uplifted and science is too dull and rationalistic? Not at all. As the Oxford professor Richard Dawkins says,

> Uplift is where science really comes into its own . . . this feeling of spine-shivering, breath-catching awe . . . this flooding of the chest with ecstatic wonder. . . . [It's] beyond the wildest dreams of saints and mystics. . . . The merest glance through a microscope at the brain of an ant or through a telescope at a long-ago galaxy of a billion worlds is enough to render poky and parochial the very psalms of praise.

Carl Sagan goes even further and claims, as so many of us might, that science is "a profound source of spirituality." He writes, "When we recognize our place in an immensity of light-years and in the passage of ages, when we grasp the intricacy, beauty, and subtlety of life, then that soaring feeling, that sense of elation and humility combined, is surely spiritual."

The marriage of science and religion. No problem for us. We're in awe, we're respectful of the evidence, we're in touch with our ability to reason. It all works fine, but it only works fine until your baby dies, until you want to find a sense of meaning in your life, until you feel anxious or confused, until you feel so good about life that you just want to explode. When you want to have a wedding, what help is science? When you're moved to celebrate the season or you feel at home in the universe, who needs empirical observation? When you want your children to learn to do the right thing, who cares what's verifiable? When you need a hug, or a metaphorical swift kick, or a little advice or reassurance; when you wonder what's valuable, really, and if your priorities are where you want them; when you want help living in a world that offers up some pretty tough days; or you want somebody to hear about the incredible feeling you had when you made it to the mountaintop; when you're looking for any of that, you're not going to turn to your high school chemistry book or the PBS science show on how lasers really work. You've got a religion to come to that's more than scientific; you've got a religion that's going to be there for you.

Religion has a big assignment. Comfort. Compassion. Fun. Nurturing the life of the spirit. Quiet. Inspiration. Motivation. Support for the children. Friendship.

And along with all of that, you've got science and reason. Add them to the wonderful mix of religion. Include them with the friendly faces you need, and the poetry, and the music. Bring your reason along with your humility and your hope and your love. Bring it along with your questions about right and wrong and how to live your life. Bring it on in with your wonderment at the connections you feel and your sense of humor. Bring that reason in with your children and your altar decorations and your shyness and your hungers and your happiness. Bring it all on in.

Science and religion? No problem.

Drawing the Breath of Life

The seasons are changing. New life and leaves in the Northern Hemisphere, autumn color in the Southern. It's on our minds and a part of our spirits. And so I think of this piece by Rev. Clarke Wells:

> I suppose I should write something institutional or churchly or ethical, but my heart isn't in it. Where my heart is these days is between me and God, or whoever it is that turns the seasons and lays the sun across the trees with that sudden and terrible beauty.
>
> I've been taught all my life to believe that growing up meant to become less vulnerable, that getting overwhelmed by life is what happens when you are young, that the charge of visions, feelings and nameless longing gradually spends itself in the process of maturing, that as we get older life is less tearing, not as confusing, ecstatic, strange.
>
> I am here to testify to the opposite and to warn myself and others about what life has in store. I was driving back from Lowell yesterday afternoon on some country roads, and I simply had to stop the car near a stone fence and go through the woods for an hour.
>
> It had nothing to do with practical matters or politics or theology or vocation or marriage

or my maturity or immaturity. It had to do with autumn trees against the blue and shattering light and where I am with living. I report it to you on the chance that you're as odd as I—that it all gets more intense, not less—so that if you have to go through the same thing, like stopping your car for an hour, you will not feel crazy, at your age, being torn apart that way.

This sermon is supposed to be about Ralph Waldo Emerson, and there's a lot I could say about his perspectives on self-reliance or American scholarship or nature. But really, I want to highlight only one of Emerson's messages, and it's the same one that Clarke Wells describes. It has nothing to do with practical matters or politics or theology or vocation or marriage or maturity or immaturity. It has to do with autumn trees against the blue and shattering light.

Emerson and the Transcendentalists who joined him—their whole deal was "direct experience," first-hand knowledge. Emerson wants you, on your way home from today's errands, to experience the season's air and the particular smell of the leaves and the stillness of time and whatever it is you might, at the end of the day, feel moved by. He would not want you to take his word for the glories all about, or my word, or the word of a religious tradition, or the word of a philosopher or poet.

We have here an Emerson who sounds for all the world like a raving New Ager. He says that the highest, most trustworthy knowledge consists of intuitive graspings, of moments of direct perception. And do you know what he calls that? He calls this process of intuiting and perceiving, "reason."

Somehow I have always assumed that most people the world over who go to high school have to read Emerson—that we all kind of grow up with him. But that's not true at all. Thinking back on it, I didn't ever learn about Emerson in school; I learned about him in my Unitarian Sunday school in Ohio. And my children didn't learn about him in school either; they learned about him in Sunday school too.

But if you did learn about Emerson in school, you probably pictured him as a cool and dispassionate commentator. A cold, white, plaster cast. A deep, aloof thinker, free of human emotion. A convoluted, eloquent, and, well, boring writer, obsessed with individualism and reason. A very smart guy, but not a lot of fun.

However, as Robert Richardson says in *Emerson: The Mind on Fire*,

> Freed of his vast, unfortunate, and self-perpetuating reputation, Emerson steps forth as a complicated, energetic, and emotionally intense man who habitually spoke against the status quo and in favor of whatever was wild and free. [He] turns out to have been a good neighbor, an activist citizen, a fond father, a loyal brother, and a man whose many friendships framed his life.

Indeed, it has been said that Emerson had more friends than any person in America. (His sister-in-law called them "Waldo's menagerie.") One author describes him as a somewhat silly youth, a lovesick suitor, and an awkward Unitarian minister; a loyal brother and grief-stricken father, a generous friend and selfless enabler of younger writers, an outraged abolitionist and vehement fomenter of civil disobedience. He also had deep feelings in favor of women's rights.

Though we have been taught to think of Emerson as an individualist, in fact he was as committed as any of us to his community in Concord, Massachusetts: He served on the school committee, the cemetery committee, the library committee, and the Lyceum committee. On specific issues he wrote letters, collared friends, addressed meetings, and signed petitions.

As a high school kid, you may have heard about what Emerson called "self-reliance." You may have picked up the more subtle distinctions, but I always took this to mean responsible. Self-reliant—as in knowing how to fry an egg or change a tire or get a load of laundry from washer to dryer and back into the drawers. And this proponent of self-reliance, this Ralph Waldo Emerson, was a fellow who had somebody else do his cooking, somebody else chop his wood, somebody else wash his clothes, while he, the self-reliant individualist, sat in his chair, surrounded by an extensive support network of family and friends, and read Goethe. It never occurred to me that Emerson wasn't talking about any of that; he was never advocating isolation or self-sufficiency. In fact, he said just the opposite: "Every being in nature has its existence so connected with other beings that if set apart from them it would instantly perish." Emerson was not telling me that I should isolate myself in an "I Am a Rock, I Am an Island" stance, but rather that I should rely on myself, my self-reliant self, for religious experiences, for spirituality.

I cut out a little story by Thomas Lee from the *New York Times* that goes like this:

An older gentleman watched me judiciously selecting pears at Dean & DeLuca recently. "How do you tell when they'll be ripe?" he asked.

"Well," I replied, "it's hard to say: a day, maybe two."

"But how do you know? I never get pears; I never know when they'll be ripe."

I passed on someone else's wise words about there being only ten perfect moments in the life of a pear and then, rather sternly, I added my own philosophy: "When the pear is ready, you have to be ready."

The gentleman looked longingly at the fruit in my basket, then timidly chose two pears from the pile in front of him. When they were bagged and weighed, he handed me his business card.

"Look," he said, "when yours are ready, will you call me?"

Know your own pears. Emerson's not going to take some stranger's word for pear ripeness. In fact, he's not even going to take the word of the owner of the grocery store! He's going to rely on his own senses and experience and intuition. "Even in a world of objective knowledge," he says, "the subjective consciousness and the conscious subject can never be left out of the reckoning." That's Transcendentalism: immediate personal experience.

And that's what Ralph Waldo Emerson, the Unitarian, contributed to our movement. He had been a minister at Second Church in Boston, where he didn't just get into hot water theologically. He was a goofus as a pastor, setting off to make pastoral calls without detailed directions, and therefore spending time visiting complete strangers who had the same name or lived on the same street as a parishioner. And if he did find the right parishioner, he was so awkward in his role as minister that at least one person just sent him away: "If you don't know your business, you had better go home."

He had trouble with the Unitarian church of the day—with communion, for example—and with the Bible, as you might imagine. He wanted direct experiences of religion for his parishioners, not set rituals like communion, symbolic of the experiences of other people long ago. And the Bible—reports of the religious experiences of antiquity—wasn't much better. Every day, right now, was blessed; every person needed to have his or her own epiphanies. "Why," he says, "should not we have a poetry and philosophy of insight and not of tradition, and a religion by revelation to us, and not the history of theirs?" "Why should we grope among the dry bones of the past? The sun shines today also." Emerson resigned as minister of the Second Church in Boston.

A few years later, a committee of students at Harvard Divinity School asked him to come and speak. It was a Unitarian seminary back then, and the students were all a-dither because Abner Kneeland, a Universalist minister, had begun serving a jail term for blasphemy. Emerson was also happy to break with the theological establishment, and he did not disappoint the students. The "Divinity School Address," one of our most important Unitarian historical events, delivered in 1838, suggests that the holy is all around us. The address begins: "In this refulgent summer, it has been a luxury to draw the breath of life." We are each religious beings, we each have religious inclinations and intuitions of our own. Religion is revealed to each person; it cannot be had second hand.

You hear that kind of talk, all these many years later, in Unitarian Universalism. Our children in Sunday school do not simply admire the crocuses that grown-ups planted; they plant them themselves, in the dirt, and with their own eyes they watch them grow in the spring. In most of our churches we do not have stained glass windows depicting religious figures through whom we derive our religious experiences; we have clear glass in the windows so a person can see out, directly to nature, in living color. These are our miracles; this is our mysticism. Emerson reassures us that spirituality is accessible to anyone who has ever sat beneath a tree on a fine clear day and looked at the world with a sense of momentary peace and a feeling, however transient, of being at one with it.

Some months ago I saw a review of the Cantata Singers in the paper. The headline read, "Cantata Singers inspired by lucid mystical powers." "Who," I wondered, "would ever put the words 'lucid' and 'mystical' next to each other in a headline or anywhere else?" Well, I think that's the kind of thing Emerson might do.

In the continuing spirit of the oracle of Concord, Ralph Waldo Emerson, again the words of Clarke Wells:

I suppose I should write something institutional or churchly or ethical, but my heart isn't in it. Where my heart is these days is between me and God, or whoever it is that turns the seasons and lays the sun across the trees with that sudden and terrible beauty.

It has nothing to do with theology. It has to do with autumn trees against the blue and shattering light and where I am with living.

Fans of Truth

"Jaws was entirely a fiction. . . . Sharks don't target human beings, and they certainly don't hold grudges. There's no such thing as a rogue man-eater shark with a taste for human flesh. In fact, sharks rarely take more than one bite out of people, because we're so lean and unappetizing to them." This from the author of *Jaws*, Peter Benchley. Having created a horror of sharks in millions of people the world over, Benchley spent the rest of his life as a global shark protectionist, still incredulous that the public couldn't distinguish fiction from truth.

For a long time, truth has been a big deal for Unitarian Universalists. It even shows up in our third principle: "A free and responsible search for truth and meaning." Like most UUs, I am a major fan of truth. But its popularity in UU circles at the moment seems to have been somewhat eclipsed by spirituality and transformation. Not totally, though.

Remember Dan Brown's novel *The Da Vinci Code*? A number of Unitarian Universalist ministers preached about it. And you know what? All of our ministers took the same approach. They asked, "What in *The Da Vinci Code* is true?" Or, "Does it matter what is true?" One way or another, what UUs cared about was truth.

"Was Jesus' 'real message' systematically distorted and hidden by the Church?" "Did Jesus really love Mary Magdalene the best and frequently kiss her on the mouth in public?" "Is it true that they had children?" "Did secret societies commit themselves to preserving Church secrets?" On some level, UUs want the facts, the truth.

But we know that religious truth is not that simple. Beyond consideration of factual truths, our ministers talked about the perils of historical subjectivity, the importance of balance, the philosophical complexities of Absolute Truth, relative truth, and postmodern truth (or the lack thereof). Who's the final arbiter? Which religious truths should we care about? Does my truth have to be your truth?

Most religion is perceived to be soft on empirical truth. Stereotypically, it depends on *truthiness*—a devotion to information that one wishes were true even if it's not. Its devotees are those who "know with their heart" instead of "thinking with their head." A phony word coined by the pretend newscaster Stephen Colbert on Comedy Central, the word truthiness has offered us a wake-up call. To remain titillated in horror by every type of shark would be a truthiness problem. Ditto for those who believe every word of *The Da Vinci Code*.

Wouldn't it be great if Unitarian Universalism could offer a nice system for establishing truth? Or degree of truth? Or the importance on a cosmic scale of any particular truth? I would really appreciate it if we could sort out the relative merits of truth in the face of hope and happiness, or hope and happiness in the face of truth. Plenty of other religions have done all this for themselves, but Unitarian Universalists, by choice, won't accomplish it anytime soon.

And that's because, ironically, we are always actively searching for truth. We welcome new evidence, new perspectives, reliable revelation. For just that reason we refuse to codify our truths into doctrine or creed; we refuse to freeze our religion in time. That's our way, and it's certainly my preference, whether the topic is sharks or religion.

What Are You Going to Be?

Halloween is coming up. You get to decide who you want to be. At least for Americans, that's a common childhood memory, and plenty of adults continue to "be" someone for Halloween. In mainstream American culture, answering the question, "What are you going to be?" occurs once a year on October 31st. For Unitarian Universalists, it's a question for every day.

We're a religion that's all about freedom. From the very beginning—as early as the fourth century—our theological forebear Pelagius denied the doctrine of original sin and taught that everyone has an inherent capacity for making free choices. In 431 the church condemned Pelagianism, but our little theological thread held on. Here we are today, Pelagians still. The outlook got a boost in the 1600s from Arminius, who again proposed that people have free will—in fact, in the early days in Massachusetts, Unitarians were called Arminians. And here we are today, Arminians still. (As my colleague Mark Belletini puts it, "Institutionally, first we were Alexandrian Origenists, then Arians, then Pelagians, then Arians again, then Erigenist Origenists, then Free Spiriters, then Antitrinitarians, then radical rational Anabaptist Christians, then Arians again, then Socinians, then Dissenters, then Arminian Dissenters, then Unitarian Christians, then Unitarian Christians again in other countries, then Unitarians, then Universalists too, then Free Associationists, then Unitarians and Universalists, then Unitarian Universalists.)

Any way you slice it, we don't need "saving"; we can choose to devote ourselves to the best purposes that we can. We are free to decide what we want to be, and not just on Halloween.

This puts the pressure on. If our destiny is not sealed, if we aren't born in sin, what's to keep us from our best selves? Where did the excuses go?

Well, there are some qualifiers. Obviously, we are only free to make choices within the confines of . . . reality. There are economics to consider, and geography, and histories of oppression, and genetics, and luck, to mention only a few factors. Some of us are born with a head start; others have indisputable barriers to overcome. No matter how free I feel, I will not be playing football for the New England Patriots. There's no way I could write a world-class symphony, nor do I have the nerves or the know-how to rob a bank. But I could choose to run for public office, teach skiing again, or sport a dramatic tattoo. While some among us defy all odds—witness the entry of the Jamaican bobsled team into the Winter Olympics some years back—most of us live where we live and do what we can.

We begin with what we begin with, and whatever the case, each of us does have significant power to "make ourselves up," to determine not only who we want to dress up as, but who we want to be. Nik Cohen puts it this way in *The Rolling Stone History of Rock & Roll*:

"Conceive, as a basis, that every life is shaped by two crucial inventions. The first is imposed from outside, at birth and during childhood . . . , the second is projected from within, as the life picks up momentum, by force of will and imagination. So we begin by being invented and we progress, if we can, to invent ourselves. The decisive element is nerve—how much . . . do we dare?"

Religiously, we're talking about more here than bobsleds and tattoos, though admittedly, they're both plenty daring. When we speak of a religious tradition that embraces freedom, we're referring to a free life of the spirit: What will you believe, how will you nourish your beliefs, how will you live your beliefs?

I just spent an afternoon in the dentist's chair. Waiting was involved, so I got a chance to get acquainted with Brian, the dental student assisting. Brian was great. He asked me what I did for a living, and he didn't flinch when I told him. He had never heard of Unitarian Universalism and he asked probing questions, listening carefully to my answers. Brian is a Mormon.

If the questions at hand are "What will you believe, how will you nourish your beliefs, how will you live your beliefs?" members of the LDS Church and Unitarian Universalists will respond with wildly different answers. Brian seemed to have an easier time of it. What does he believe? Mormon doctrine, of course. The beliefs are listed right on their website under "The truth about life's great questions is now restored." How does he nourish his beliefs? He spends his time with other Mormons.

How does he live his beliefs? Well, his church sets that out pretty clearly.

My own answers included the Unitarian Universalist's responsibility to develop sustaining, inspiring, ethical beliefs that spur us to action and good will. We are fed by our work in the world, our communities, and our inner lives. We try to act according to the best that our consciences have to offer.

Brian was astonished to hear the extent of Unitarian Universalist freedom. To him we seemed, well, daring. To his credit, he maintained a non-anxious presence, but I could tell he was worried, and I tried to reassure him that it really works out fine.

Many of our congregations sing a hymn that goes like this: "Since what we choose is what we are, and what we love we yet shall be, the goal may ever shine afar—the will to win it makes us free."

That's our heritage. That's the challenge—to figure out who you're going to be—not only for Halloween, but all the time.

Corn and Chaff Together

Unitarian Universalists are known for our upbeat religion. Our babies are not born into original sin—we believe children are terrific from the get-go. When the cycle of life completes itself, we're up-beat still. Our tendency is toward memorial services, where the dead are not present, and life is celebrated as much as is possible, given our loss.

So when we hear a poem like Wislawa Szymborska's "A Word on Statistics," maintaining the decidedly upbeat viewpoint is tough. The poem proposes statistics about the human condition and they are not the statistics I want to believe. She estimates "Capable of happiness," at "twenty-some-odd" percent at most, for instance, when I want to see it way up in the 90s. And couldn't the poem please give "Ready to help" at least a 95, or even the full 100 percent? Nope, it's at 49. I want to see high numbers for "good" and "wise"; low for "cruel" and "balled up in pain," but the poet does the reverse.

In fact, it's in our religious communities where I most want my wishful stats to be true. Wouldn't it be great if churches could be one place where everything is perfect? Where we admire and empathize and always are just? Where all lives are happy and wise, where spiritual emptiness is filled? A congregation where everyone finds meaning and purpose, where every dream, every plan, every expectation or vision of life pans out—a congregation of perfect people, a heavenly place on earth, peopled with saints?

Our ancestors tried this plan. It didn't work out. In one branch of our Unitarian Universalist religious family tree we find the Puritans, from whom we broke away. And the way the Puritans had it figured, there were two kinds of people: the good people—themselves—and the bad people. The Puritans didn't much like the bad people, or sin, or wickedness for that matter, and so in 1630, there in England, they packed themselves up and took off for a hemisphere that was pure.

But somehow, after living in the Massachusetts Bay Colony for awhile, undeniably, everyone was not pure, and it wasn't completely obvious which people were the good people and which were the wicked ones. If you want a church full of only perfect people, "visible saints," they called them, you have to devise a test. Which, by 1640, they did.

Say you want to join the Puritan church. You interview with the church elders, who examine your religious knowledge and religious experience. If you are ignorant, graceless, or scandalous, you are turned back then and there. But if you pass that test, all the church members begin to ask around about you, to snoop, to uncover possible moral offenses. If, after all that, you can get church members to testify to your good behavior, you have the opportunity to describe to the gathered congregation the way in which God's saving grace came to you. Then you are questioned by the congregation at large. Once that's over, you make a public profession of faith, in your own words. Then there's a vote. (One fellow I read about got

61

nearly all the way through, then heard himself say that saving grace had come to him "while he was enjoying a pipe of the good creature tobacco." He was, as they say, history.) All that—that was the "test."

We didn't stick with this strategy of visible saints. One of our forbears of the period, John Eliot, thought that purity of membership was for the birds. He believed we have a responsibility to mix with, as he put it, "sinners and heathens." He figured churches should admit everyone, "so as to keep the whole heape of chaff and corne together."

We have adopted John Eliot's position, "chaff and corne together," some of us taking the role of corn one week, only to have a week as chaff the next. Of course, that's not how we've come to see it—corn and chaff, good and bad—but rather people together, a religious community of folks who understand the pleasure and pain of living on this planet.

We have come to understand that Szymborska's numbers, at least the ones at the very end of her poem, are worthy of our attention and our embrace. She says those who deserve empathy are ninety-nine percent. And, "Mortal: one hundred out of one hundred—a figure that has never varied yet."

The Lure of Dinette Sets

I am eight years old, or maybe eleven, watching "The Price is Right" game show on TV. Probably I have the sniffles or something and am home from school. I am an American child being enculturated, watching and learning how grown-ups behave. I take this show seriously.

What is expected of adults, I'm wondering? These grown-ups get to be on national television—what do they know about, care about? What do I need to learn?

Bill Cullen, the show's original host, invited contestants to "Come on down." And did they ever! They'd see a potential prize—a refrigerator or room-full of furniture—and the hopefuls tried to guess the retail price. Whoever came closest without going over won the prize. As I say, I somehow took this show seriously, even without knowing that "The Price is Right" would become the longest running TV game show in American television history.

The elementary questions I was asking, there with the sniffles, were questions that are answered in most cultures by religion. What are our fundamental values? What's the canon, the body of lore that we need to incorporate into our being in order to become fully functioning adults in our society? What does "getting it right" look like? Some children my age memorized verses of the Quran, learned the stories in the Christian scriptures, focused on the Five Books of Moses at yeshivas, were being introduced to the disciplines of yoga. But I was watching "The Price is Right," memorizing the prices of washing machines and fur coats and dinette sets. I tried to learn to care about them, to want them. I practiced jumping up and down and squealing in case, if I were really on the show someday, I won the lawn mower, or the china place settings, service for eight. Not to mention the grand piano or the odd bonus prizes, a sixteen-foot Ferris wheel, one hundred pounds of Swiss cheese, or even an actual elephant. The elephant would definitely require some screeches of delight.

But Sundays roll around, and in our family we always went to Sunday school at our local Unitarian Universalist fellowship. While "The Price is Right," or the stock market, or any number of consumer pastimes can become something like a religion, the Fellowship offered a corrective —another model for what grown-ups cared about, how I might behave, what I needed to know to grow up in our culture.

Neither the building nor the religion was particularly fancy. Both were functional though, and completely in line with a quote I found in my great-grandfather's book of Unitarian sermons: "I know that religion sends me out into the world with a stronger inclination to display a good will, a just, honest, helpful will than I should have without it. Such is the leading test." This was not the world that Bill Cullen lived in, nor later, Bob Barker. The Fellowship offered a world where adults just got together and tried to be better people. At least that's how it looked to me.

Peter Berger's *The Sacred Canopy* came out about then, in which he says that people sometimes forget how to behave. "They must, therefore, be reminded over and over again. Indeed, it may be argued that one of the oldest and most important prerequisites for the establishment of culture is the institution of such reminders."

I know now that there's more to religion than that. It's broader and deeper than a tap on the shoulder and a reminder about the Golden Rule. Yet I do need to be reminded to lead with the assumption of good will, to do everything I can to live simply and save the planet, to make a little space for gratitude and calm. It really helps to have this religion, this Unitarian Universalism, with its unabashed focus on lives here and now, its encouragement for grounding in goodness and health, its constant reminders that we have work to do in the world. It is not the only religion, it is not the perfect religion, but as Rev. Minot Simons said just over one hundred years ago in my old book, it's a religion that sends me out into the world with a stronger inclination to display a good will, a more just, honest, and helpful will than I would otherwise have.

I have not watched "The Price is Right" in many decades, though I know it's still on and—who knows—I might like it a lot. But I'm glad for religion's tug, reminding me always that in spite of the possible lure of dinette sets, Unitarian Universalism offers me more.

Not Perfect Yet?

The email's subject line was simple: "Confession."

Confession. It's a creepy little word. You don't know what the email's going to say. Am I about to learn that the author gained access to a congregation's stock portfolio, and, well, made off with it, but would feel better telling me on the way out of town? Or am I about to learn only that the emailer ate three cupcakes, one right after the other? Maybe it's going to have something to do with the IRS. Or sex. Or how bad a fellow can feel having had the dog neutered. Confession.

Here it was, an apparent electronic confession from my old Star Island friend, Tom Stites, formerly the editor of the *UU World*. It made sense, come to think of it. We'd had a conversation about—that's right—confession. He'd observed that all religions provide for confession. He'd mentioned that, having been raised Episcopalian, he missed something in our Unitarian Universalist services that regularly acknowledges our short-comings. Of course I had responded in a sensitive, pastoral manner: "You've got to be kidding!" I said. "We're Unitarian Universalists! We don't believe in original sin. Quite the opposite— we believe in taking responsibility for our behavior. We believe that we can change for the better, that we aren't bad people—we just have some growing to do."

But, of course, Tom was right. I checked. Every major religion confesses, repents. The Quran, for example, says,

"To those who repent . . . , and make amends—God is All-forgiving, All-compassionate."

The Hindu hymn to the god Varuna pleas, "Loose me from sin as from a bond that binds me. . . . What, Varuna, hath been my chief transgression . . . ? Tell me, unconquerable Lord, and quickly sinless will I approach thee with my homage."

The Hebrew scriptures are clear on the topic: "When you realize your guilt . . . , you shall confess the sin that you have committed. The priest shall make atonement on your behalf for the sin that you have committed, and you shall be forgiven."

Finally, in the Christian scriptures, we know that Jesus begins his ministry with a call to repentance and an acknowledgment of sin as a condition of divine forgiveness.

Well, as Unitarian Universalists, we pretty much haven't done any of that.

We've always had a different spin on sin. The Universalists believed (and I'm quoting from the early nineteenth-century leader Hosea Ballou) that "There is nothing in heaven above, nor in the earth beneath, that can do away with sin—but Love." A shocking point of view.

If God loves us as we are, so the logic went among early Unitarians and Universalists, where would confession come in?

Well, I can tell you what I think: We're not perfect yet. Personally, I'm not always so pleased with myself. I'm not satisfied. I want to do better, to *be* better. To contribute more, to detract less; to be more on the side of justice and less on the side of complacency; to understand more fully; to love more easily. It can be discouraging, living a life, and that's worth saying out loud.

So I read the email from my friend Tom, the message labeled "Confession." It was not about embezzlement, chocolate cupcakes, or the IRS. He said, "The following is the confession I wrote as an assignment we had in Kansas City in our 'Building Your Own Theology' class at church." Here's the confession—Tom gave me permission to share it:

In this ritual of healing and cleansing, we acknowledge our imperfections and confess to ourselves, and publicly to each other, that we have fallen short in the crucial effort to live lives worth dying for.

We have allowed minutiae and unimportant things to rule our lives and to claim precious hours that should be devoted to concerns that are important to us, to our families and friends, and to the communities that sustain all our lives.

We have given too much power to fears and anger and pain.

And in focusing too much on our own wants, we have arrogantly presumed that, despite overwhelming evidence of the vastness of the universe and the infinite sweep of time, we have special importance.

Let us rejoice that in each of us is the power to improve not only ourselves but also the needy world of which we are citizens. Let us seize this moment to renew our commitments to doing the right things and the important things, to confronting our fears, and to bowing in respect to the mysteries of nature.

As a Unitarian Universalist, Tom's is a confession that I can wrap my mind around! But . . .

Catholics, having confessed, receive absolution from the priest. Jews, after much soul-searching during the High Holy Days, begin again with a fresh start. Unitarian Universalists?

Well, as a group, we don't have the post-confession stage worked out. To regain a peaceful state of mind, some of us walk, or write in our journals, or talk with friends, or straighten it out in therapy, or we meditate. Others simply find that having confessed—having honestly acknowledged our own shortcomings either privately or in the presence of another person—the day comes when unexpectedly, the burden is lifted.

In the end, ours is a positive religion, with primary focus on all that is good, wondrous, and just. Yet we are not so different from everybody else in the need to confess, to feel sorry, and to begin again with hope. We leave room for that too.

What Holds Us Together?

One summer, my friend Rev. Barbara Merritt and her husband took their family to Nova Scotia for a vacation. They wound up in a place called Digby Neck—maybe some of you have been there. Well, Digby Neck has what they call an "amethyst beach," where, according to the Canadian tourist literature, you can collect your own amethysts. The Merritt family decided this would be a wonderful family project, something they could all do together. They were given directions to the beach, down several unmarked roads, and one of the locals told them to "look for the boulders of black volcanic rock. On the surface of those rocks, you'll find white lines, the cracks where the crystals form. When you can locate the larger cavities of crystals, you'll be harvesting amethyst."

Barbara grabbed a large canvas bag to haul back all the semi-precious gemstones, and off they went. She says,

> Putting all our heads together we found the beach, the black smooth volcanic rock, and the white lines. We brought along hammers and safety goggles and went to work. An hour later we were still smashing at rocks, for no apparent reason. Deep within the white crystal cracks, we discovered a lot of . . . rock.
>
> We each had our own strategies for searching. Initially I scanned the boulders for visual clues of

hidden caches of amethyst. I'd make a thoughtful scientific appraisal of the area, following fault lines, looking for subtle gradations in color, listening for hollow echoes with my hammer. At each spot where I finally chose to chip away, my hopes were high. I was sure that this was it! It wasn't.

Later I decided to use my intuition. I "opened" myself to the presence of amethyst; I tried to become emotionally in tune with the geological harmony of the place. I attempted to be "guided" to the right spot. When everything felt just right, I'd strike with the hammer. And lo and behold, underneath the surface, were more rocks!

One can expectantly smash rocks on a beach for only so long. Though we were models of mutual encouragement, my husband and children had fared no better than I had. We had each made premature declarations that we were about to break open the mother lode of amethyst. The canvas sack remained empty. . . .

As we were leaving the beach . . . I saw, out of the corner of my eye, a small piece of black rock. I picked it up, turned it over, and I saw it! A faint pinkish cast to the crystals. (You might not see it, but there was definitely some pink there.) I tucked it in my pocket, and went on my way.

Well now, there's an analogy. One could apply it a lot of ways. In a job search—you hammer here, chip away there, with high hopes for the semiprecious benefits package. Certainly you could apply it to dating—you look here and there, under the rocks, breaking through the tough exteriors, hoping to bag that perfect gem. Perhaps it even applies to shopping for a church, where maybe, if you look hard enough, some church will show itself where the theology is exactly right and everybody's life goes according to plan. But naturally, I am drawn to apply the analogy to Unitarian Universalism.

I like it. Unitarian Universalists, all there together on Amethyst Beach, take our little hammers and try to uncover the truth for ourselves about, say, the afterlife. Then we move to another spot, chip away a little, and try to expose some truth about inner peace. Another spot, an investigation of a personal question of ethics, or a fine point of theology, or a practical question about teaching the Hindu concept of reincarnation in Sunday school, or basic questions about what comes next. We're always there, all of us together, with our little hammers.

The problem quickly comes with the "empty canvas bag" portion of the analogy. We do a lot of hammering, but Barbara Merritt is quite right that "One can expectantly smash rocks on a beach for only so long." After searching for most of a lifetime, wouldn't a person expect to find some gigantic, impressive amethyst? After engaging in the religious search year after year, wouldn't a person expect to discover the absolute truth about life after death, or the perfect method of teaching Sunday school, or the most tranquil of tranquilities? Why, after all these years with the little hammer, is the canvas bag so . . . light?

I mean, doesn't that strike you as odd? A religion of people who, metaphorically speaking, gather on a beach, searching and searching but never actually hauling home that great and heavy bag full of answers?

Well, let's keep this analogy going just a little longer. True, most of us don't ever collect that big amethyst. But after a while, we do find a lovely collection of stones that bear, for us, the pinkish hue of truth. We fill our pockets with spiritual insight, aphorisms, moral clarity, poignant story, personal encounter, or quiet moments of peace. Most of us feel fine with the security of those rock fragments clunking away in our pockets.

But the further question presents itself about Unitarian Universalism: "If we're each out there on the beach wandering around searching, what holds us together in Unitarian Universalist community?"

I have heard this question all my life. When I was in elementary school, now and then a friend would ask, "How can you have a religion if you don't all believe the same thing?" So I asked my mom what I could answer, and she said, "Tell them that in our church, we don't think alike, we walk together." That seemed about right to me, because already from Sunday school I knew that different children in the class believed different things, but still we were the same group as we moved from one grade to the next.

Later, in high school, when I was sixteen and knew everything, I learned three words: *demographics*, *self-select*, and *theological*. By then, if anyone had the misfortune of asking me what held the people in Unitarian Universalist churches together, I would say, very pretentiously I'm afraid, "It's not so much a matter of theology, we tend to self-select demographically." By this I simply meant that we were the smart people, the people who questioned and developed our own opinions about matters of religion.

Mercifully, I didn't stick with that response all that long. Before I knew it college was behind me, I was twenty-two years old, I was in theological school, and I began to realize that better minds than mine had wrestled with this question, and that the answers were written down.

Unitarians and Universalists have a long history of covenanting with one another—of literally articulating what it is that holds us together. A few of you grew up with such a covenant in your church—maybe James Vila Blake's "Love is the spirit of this church, and service its law. This is our great covenant: To dwell together in peace, To seek the truth in love, And to help one another." Congregational covenants are one approach to the problem of holding us together.

Looking for a broader approach, delegates to the Unitarian Universalist Association's General Assemblies in the 1980s voted to adopt Principles and Purposes as a part of the Association's bylaws. Not a creed, not a statement of doctrine, not a personal theology, this statement, revised in 1995, reminds us that member Unitarian Universalist congregations (though not necessarily individuals) have a common approach to religion.

Of course, any of us can simply sit down and type out what we believe holds Unitarian Universalists together—for personal clarification or because we're constantly hearing the comment, "Those Unitarian Universalists don't believe in anything. What holds them together?" In the words of a former president of the Unitarian Universalist Association, Rev. Bill Schulz, "This is the mission of our faith: To teach the fragile art of hospitality; To revere both the critical mind and the generous heart; To prove that diversity need not mean divisiveness; And to witness to all that we must hold the whole world in our hands."

Just the other day, after a lifetime of hearing it, I heard the question again: "You're a Unitarian Universalist minister. Tell me, if you don't have a doctrine, what holds you all together?" Well, what *does* hold us together?!

Thankfully, I've been around a while, so I have files. Lots of files. And you know, every UU minister on the planet has a little something to say about what holds us together: It's hope. It's love. Freedom. The pursuit of truth. Diversity itself. Concern for one another's well-being. Community. Beauty. Connectedness. Mystery. You can post these essays all over the room, all over the house really—I have dozens—you can read them off and on all day, and still you can wake up the next morning, scratch your head, and ask yourself, "What does hold us together?"

Here's what I think. We don't have a doctrine or a creed. But we have a history. It's those Pilgrims again.

Early on, the Pilgrims covenanted together to search in freedom for spiritual truths. Put in modern language, their covenant says, "We pledge to walk together in the ways of truth and affection, as best we know them now or may learn them in days to come, that we and our children may be fulfilled and that we may speak to the world in words and actions of peace and goodwill."

That's what my mother told me to say when I was nine: "What holds Unitarians and Universalists together?" "We promise not to think alike but to walk together." She used the same words the Pilgrims used.

Walking together. This is our heritage. This is what holds us together. In the words of Rev. Alice Blair Wesley,

> This is the spirit of our people. It is holy to us, this walking together. It holds us all . . . insofar as we live by it, in the embrace of the free church, in the generous embrace of people who are centered—in ever-changing and responsively creative ways—around a promise of searching for and daring to live by truth.

That's what we try to do together as members and friends in Unitarian Universalist congregations.

Sounds a little like what a family might do on an amethyst beach, doesn't it? Everybody together, there on the beach, exploring, searching, checking the cracks and crevices. Pretty soon we forget, mostly, about the canvas bag. It wasn't all that important anyway. The few pink-hued rock chips tucked into the pocket are enough in the gemstone department, and the day on the beach with the other searchers was—well, what a day it was. Held together by the search, walking together.

Who Gets to Be Right?

Depending on where you are from and the people your family liked to spend time with, as a child you may have spent Saturday nights or Sunday afternoons listening to groups of adults who were Lebanese cab drivers, or Yankee potato farmers, or Socialist Jews from New York City, or entrepreneurs in Hong Kong. Maybe you grew up among Fundamentalist Christians.

I didn't, exactly. But I did grow up in rural Ohio, in a Mormon ("Reorganized Church of Jesus Christ of Latter Day Saints") town, and our family was the one Unitarian family. I know this isn't what your encyclopedia will tell you, but in school, and on the street, and in Camp Fire Girls, and at basketball practice, and everywhere we went, we learned that the good guys established the settlement and the Kirtland temple. And in 1832 the bad guys tarred and feathered Joseph Smith and ran him out of town. That's how religion works. Simple as that.

Where I grew up, we didn't hear a word about respect for theological pluralism. There was no such thing as interfaith dialogue, or many paths to one truth, or anything like that. My friends all knew what Joseph Smith had said and they believed every word: "Truth is Mormonism. God is the author of it." In 1958, Rev. Phil Giles said, on behalf of the Universalist Church of the Larger Fellowship, "The word *liberal* has been used constantly as a term of opprobrium, particularly since the rise of

Neo-orthodoxy." From personal experience, I know that this is true.

Needless to say, for the most part I grew up among earnest, kind, committed people and I am left with a special fondness for the people back home. But like some of you, I do know what it's like to live among people—friends and neighbors—who understand themselves to have the one true viewpoint, for whom dialogue as equals is not a value, and whose belief system is, frankly, unthinkable to me.

Some people are absolutists. They believe they are appointed carriers of a sacred Gospel. Those who take their faith to the extreme feel so sure they are right that they have no compunctions about doing anything to advance their cause. We saw the phenomenon in the Jewish fundamentalist Yigal Amir, who claimed that God ordered him to kill Prime Minister Rabin. We have seen Muslim fundamentalists who are willing to sacrifice their own lives and the lives of innumerable others in the name of their religion. Some Hindus massacre Muslims and blow up their mosques. Some Christians feel they are serving God by murdering doctors who perform abortions. We see people doing what they believe is the Lord's work in religious conflicts all over the world.

Mostly though, the day-to-day experience of Unitarian Universalists living in local communities with members of conservative religious traditions involves not bullets or bombs but politics, both personal and on a grander scale.

You know the platform—it's a list that stands in sharp contrast with typical Unitarian Universalist beliefs. Religious conservatives (and I am no longer talking about my childhood neighbors here) often say they know that they should obey the word of God—as spoken to them—over and above the laws of the land. They say they know abortion is always wrong. They say they know that homosexuality is an abomination in God's sight. They say they know that capital punishment is a fitting punishment. They say they know the source of authority is scripture. In the United States, they say they know we should "return to our roots as a 'Christian nation,'" and then, with stunning irony, they cite as their bedfellows Unitarian and Deist names such as Jefferson, Paine, Washington, Franklin, Madison, and John Adams.

So what are we going to do? I've heard it said a hundred times, "There's no talking to these people." But even if that were true, we have to. We just have to.

We start out knowing that we, ourselves, don't always agree. Sometimes I suppose we don't even make sense. We aren't at our best every single day, and it's not so hard to lose sight of the dignity and worth of the people around us. But still we have to talk. We have to speak up.

Even at the worst, at the risk of entering a world that we'd rather avoid, we have to try to talk. In the face of unfathomable arguments, we have to try to talk. At the risk of hate-based rhetoric, we have to try to talk. Publicly, enthusiastically, confidently, hopefully. To stand firm. Wherever we are, whoever we are.

Me? I'm not that good at it. But still, there's hope. The town I grew up in? If I went back today, I could attend a Unitarian Universalist church right there in town. It's not too far from the Mormon Temple.

Our Religion Made Manifest

Nobody cares what denomination you belong to. That's what ministers are told these days: "People couldn't care less." The best bet, say the experts, is to keep parishioners happy by emphasizing Wednesday night stress-reduction programs, divorce support groups, bridge nights, convenient parking—that sort of thing—in an up-beat and welcoming tone. "Give the consumers what they want and lure them in." Believe me, none of the articles advises the clergy ever to describe straight-up theological beliefs to members of the congregation—and certainly not the business meetings!

But I can't help myself. The thing is, our Unitarian Universalist religion is a blast! I love it. Our purposes and principles in our bylaws—aren't they pretty cool? We're talking about the dignity and worth of every person. Justice and fairness and compassion. Spiritual growth. The search for truth and meaning. The democratic process— in a church! A love of the natural world. What's not to like? We stand for something as a unique religion. If you spend much time contemplating a list like that, really, it is exciting and transforming—at least it is for me. Better than bridge.

Imagine the feeling during the summer meetings when delegates from Unitarian Universalist congregations gather at our General Assembly. You might join any group of five people, or a dozen, or a couple hundred, or thousands, and they would all be Unitarian Universalists who share the values expressed in our Principles and Purposes—more or less. This annual meeting will not be about card games or stress reduction; it will be about big-time religious issues like racial justice and healthy families. It will be about beauty and grace in religious life, about raising a new generation of children, about activism, about healing the spirit.

I can pretty much guarantee that one way or another, if you go to GA, you'll have your moments. Moments that mean something, moments of excitement and inspiration, moments of silly surprise.

I've been there, I know. In 1994, our General Assembly took place in Fort Worth. When I arrived, the time and temperature sign said 96 degrees. I had never seen such a high number on a time and temperature sign before, so for fun I bought a throwaway camera and took a picture of the sign. This particular sign actually flashed, "96 degrees," and then it went on to spell out the words, "Welcome Unitarian Universalist Association," followed by "Mud-Wrestling Championships." That was a moment right there, and I had only just arrived!

General Assembly is a gigantic town meeting, where representatives of congregations gather to decide what our association of churches, called the Unitarian Universalist Association, should do next. We have no pope, no hierarchy, no big guys behind the scenes making decisions for us, and consequently we have an enormous amount of democratic work cut out for us.

So the delegates are gathered there in Fort Worth, it's 100 degrees now, I'm impressed, I take another picture of the time and temperature sign while I'm deciding which programs to go to next: Japanese Unitarians, young adult networks, socially responsible investing, weaving creative space, frontiers in the science-religion relationship, money and the meaning of life, Christian communions, creative writing as feminist liberation theology, or music and sounds as tools of healing.

I decide on a workshop. I consult the program book and determine the location. I check the map, find the right building, and approach the room number. But before I open the door, I hear singing from across the hall. A huge room full of Unitarian Universalists singing—well and with pep. My workshop plan foiled, though I'm more a listener than a singer, I reverse my trajectory and follow my ears. It's not that the hymn is a particular favorite of mine, nor that I have fond childhood memories of singing it with Sunday school friends. What never fails to capture my attention at General Assembly is the simple fact of many hundreds of Unitarian Universalists singing our hymns together. I can't find that any other place.

The experience of General Assembly is like that for me, days made up of moments. Running into someone I used to know in another context. Who knew we are both UUs? Hearing a new strategy for supporting stem cell research—boom—like a lightning bolt, it makes so much sense. Proudly listening to a youth at the microphone at a plenary session, pondering a theological point that's completely new to me, engaging in hot debate over where we should put our money—not quite mud wrestling, but close. That's what's so great about General Assembly—you can walk into any room and see our religion made manifest.

I went outside on my last June evening in Fort Worth, where the time and temperature sign said "110 degrees." It's 6:30 at night and it's 110 degrees! I'm impressed. I take a final picture.

Now, years later, the pictures long lost, I've gone and done it. In spite of the experts' advice, here I am gushing about Unitarian Universalism, and our annual meeting. I hope it's contagious, and I hope to see you there.

Suddenly, We're a Band

Have you ever been reading the classifieds when you see an ad, say, for a guitarist looking for a drummer? And then a couple of ads down you see another ad, this time for a drummer looking for a guitarist? And you have the urge to call them both and do a little matchmaking?

This phenomenon caught the attention of the public radio show "This American Life." They decided to have some fun creating a band composed of musicians found in the classifieds of one issue of the *Chicago Sun-Times*. There was only one qualification: no two musicians could ever have played together "under any other imaginable circumstances."

So it was that seven musicians, complete strangers to one another, gathered in a recording studio to record what would be their one and only song. John, a country punk bandleader, gathered Ben, an indie rocker bassist, followed by an acid funk percussionist named Steve. Also listed in the classifieds that day were Nathan, an electric violinist with an "anger management problem," working on a conspiracy theory rock opera, and a smooth, soulful, sultry, female jazz vocalist named Karen. The last two to join the band were an "experienced Christian worship leader" who strummed a guitar, and Eric, a sixty-something retired factory worker who, in his ad, promised "to amaze you" with his theremin's effects.

Sound like any religion you know?

In Unitarian Universalism, the environmentalist in Illinois joins with the grocery bagger in Cheyenne and the night-owl software developer in Seattle. The incarcerated Unitarian Universalist is one of us, as is the teenager from the Bible belt who sneaks onto our websites, and the energetic retirement home resident who leads a small group of UUs in worship once a month.

Some delight in their isolation, as did the electric violinist, off alone in a corner of the recording studio. All they really want to do is support the general cause of liberal religion. Others prefer relationship; they bond as instantly as the rhythm section did in Public Radio's one-day band.

What captures my imagination, though, is the theological diversity of our membership. When we conducted one recent survey, predictably, a number of members wrote creative descriptions of their theologies:

earth-centered humanist
agnostic/Christian/nature
deist
spiritual humanist
Christian-Buddhist
theistic humanist
mystic-earth-nature centered
Gnostic
pagan, not earth-centered
Taoist
Heinz 57

naturalistic mystic
humanist-Christian
Christian-Eastern-New Age
religious naturalist
pagan

While most of us identify primarily as straight-up Unitarian Universalists, when asked, we sort ourselves most readily into the following theological subgroups: humanists, earth-centered, atheist/agnostics, theists, Christians, mystics, and Buddhists (in that order numerically). There is room for us all.

During the radio show, John, the punk bandleader, told us there wasn't enough amazement in his life. He knocked on the door of the theremin player partly because this Eric promised amazement. When Eric began to play "Danny Boy" on his theremin, waving his hand above it, never touching it, thus disturbing the electromagnetic field and creating a sound like a flying saucer from the Twilight Zone gone Irish, the band leader was truly amazed. But when the band of strangers came together and recorded Elton John's "Rocket Man," and it really sounded great, that was the clear winner of the day in the amazement department. "Suddenly," John said, "they're a band."

For us it works the same way. As individual Unitarian Universalists we are, I like to suppose, amazing. But together, when from wherever we are, we support the cause of liberal religion and all it stands for, when we ground ourselves in our solid religion, when we share Unitarian Universalism with those who need to hear about it, suddenly, we're a church.

Amazing.

God (and Variations on the Theme)

Do you believe in God?

I don't know how often you get asked. Maybe never. But every couple of months somebody asks me if I believe in God. They might ask in exactly that way, "Do you believe in God?" Or maybe, "You do believe in God, don't you?" Or, from a child perhaps, "Is there really a God?"

How do you answer? I know that some of you figure, "There's an easy question. The answer is 'Yes.'" Or "The answer is 'No.'" No problem. Another clump of you no doubt respond with something like, "It depends on what you mean by God." You want your questioner to name the terms before you make a commitment. And then another batch of you probably goes right ahead and defines your own terms—your own conception of what might be sacred from your own perspective. You say something like, "Well, I do believe in some spirit out there, or something bigger than ourselves, or that there is some larger purpose to our lives." Maybe you call that God, maybe you don't.

When somebody asks me, "Do you believe in God?" I immediately feel uneasy. Not because I feel defensive about my belief system, not even because I can't figure out why, in any given case, they might be asking. I feel uneasy because when someone asks, "Do you believe in God," I don't know what they're talking about!

They know. They know what the word *God* means, or they wouldn't ask the question in that way. And not only do they know what the word God means, they seem to understand a common definition of the word, a definition that they think I must be familiar with. But I'm not. And I'm a minister. It's weird.

So, one day, I'm standing in line at the Department of Motor Vehicles, a long line, to accomplish a routine but not-able-to-be-done-online task, and I'm reading some God-related book or other and the guy ahead of me in line asks, "Do you believe in God?" And as usual, I have no idea what he means.

When someone uses the word God there in the Department of Motor Vehicles—or in church or in a serious discussion in your living room—when someone says the word God to me, I see in my mind's eye a menu. And on that menu is a list of gods. In Sunday school I was taught, and our Unitarian Universalist congregations still teach—that if god exists, god has many faces.

So all those many faces occur to me there at the DMV in the driver's license line. "Oh dear," I wonder, "does this man mean God as love, or God as punisher, or God as nature, or God as benefactor? Is his God a Presbyterian Sunday school God, a Roman Catholic God, a Quaker God? Is he talking about the Rainbow Serpent, or Allah, or the Goddess, or Yahweh, or God the Father, or the ground of all being? Is it the God who blesses sick babies or the God who sends violent tropical storms?" I don't know.

But those aren't the kinds of questions one can ask there in the DMV (the line's not *that* long). The truth is, there are a lot of gods out there I don't believe in.

And so I say to the man in line, "I believe in big mysteries. I believe in depth of feeling—feelings so deep within the spirit that the connection, or the bliss, or the peace, stay with us forever. And I believe in a goodness, a goodness created by our love and our care."

He says, "Fine." That was all there was to it, and I went back to my book.

No, as it turned out, my companion in the line had not wanted to engage in a spirited discussion of conceptions of god. Nor did he want to recommend the many anthologies of spiritual readings available, or compendia of gods and goddesses from everywhere on earth. He didn't even want to tell me what he thought, and he certainly had no interest in listening to further observations from me!

But still, the God question is a good one, even in its short and stark form, and ideally, we should all be able to blurt out a quick response. I, for one, did not have an answer at the ready—I found it hard to synthesize my own world-view in a cogent and succinct way at the Department of Motor Vehicles.

Oddly, once we get started on articulating our views on gods, it's not so bad. One can think about hundreds of gods, gods around which whole civilizations developed, and quite readily cross them off our personal lists—I, for one, am just not going to relate, for example, to a caribou god. Closer to home, it's just as easy, for me at least, to cross off a vengeful god who punishes with earthquakes and AIDS and shootings, or a god who only loves the Baptists, or a god who would hear me if I were to pray for good weather for a wedding. Once we've narrowed it down this far, we are within the range of what most Unitarian Universalists might believe.

We can carve up Unitarian Universalist views in a number of ways. In my mind, whether we use the word *god* or not doesn't matter much. It's a word I virtually never use, what with all the confusion around it. What I'm about to say applies to atheists as much as is does to theists and agnostics.

Each of us believes something about the nature of life and the cosmos—some call whatever that is God, some describe it in other ways. That's more semantics than religion. But there are some theological categories that may be helpful. I'm going to remind you of three such categories here—obviously I could suggest a hundred or a thousand—no two Unitarian Universalists have exactly the same perspective.

But let's take the label *theism* for openers—the technical, academic term. Some of you are theists, and strictly speaking, if you are a theist, you believe four things about God: Your god is personal. For example, you can imagine your god, you can communicate with your god. Second: God merits worship and adoration because God is good and all-powerful. Third: God is separate from our world—above us, or beyond us somehow. And fourth:

God is active in our world, here and now. If you call yourself a theist, that's what religionists would expect you to believe.

A second traditional category in religion is *pantheism*. The label has never caught on in our popular culture, though I think the spirit of it has. If you believe that everything that exists is a part of a whole, a unity, and if you believe that this all-inclusive unity is in some sense divine, then you are a pantheist. For example, Matthew Fox—the Dominican priest who founded the "Creation Spirituality" movement some years back—seems to think this way. In *For the Love of God*, he says,

> I can pick up a blade of grass and experience its twenty-billion-year history and its color, shape, and form. We can feel awe when we experience the planet, or a dog, or a friend. Anything that has "being" is holy. . . . I heard Beethoven for the first time when I was in high school, and it made my soul leap. And there was . . . Shakespeare. . . . I think that most people's basic experience of God is like Einstein's—the awe of the universe, the experience of the cosmos as our home, and God dwelling there. . . . We must learn to be entranced again by the presence of God in all things.

If you tend to think that way—of connection and unity and awe all around you—you may want to consider youself a pantheist.

Or you may fit into a third category, you may be a deist. Deists believe that there had to be something, God let's say, that got the universe started in the first place. A deist will say that the cosmos is just too complex to have happened by chance. But this God is not around to supervise our day-to-day lives. Deists believe then in an "absentee God."

Benjamin Franklin, Thomas Jefferson, George Washington, and Thomas Paine were deists. In *The Age of Reform*, Thomas Paine writes,

> I believe in one God, . . . and I believe that religious duties consist in doing justice, loving mercy, and endeavoring to make our fellow-creatures happy. But, lest it be supposed that I believe many other things in addition to these, I shall . . . declare the things I do not believe: . . . I do not believe in the creed professed by the Jewish church, by the Roman church, by the Greek church, by the Turkish church, by the Protestant church, nor by any church that I know of. My own mind is my own church.

Within Unitarian Universalism, you can be, of course, a theist, a pantheist, or a deist, or you can take any other religious position that pleases your heart and satisfies your mind, including atheism. In *A History of God*, Karen Armstrong tells us that the statement "I believe in God" has no objective meaning at all, that each generation has to create the image of God that works for it. Unitarian Universalists are unified in that we are our own theologians, and the choice is ours, not once and for all, but throughout our lives.

Of course, you may not like being analytical about the experience of god, and categories don't appeal to you. For you, simple experience may say it all. When we are paying attention, miraculous moments happen in each of our lives. Some of you call that *God*.

Perhaps the concept of god does not interest you much, but you know what you do and do not believe. Or maybe your beliefs are growing and changing all the time, and it helps to attach theological labels to them along the way. Maybe you simply have a feeling of god and don't go much for talking it through. But wherever you are, whatever you believe, know that each of us has the same assignment: to name the source of our blessings, the foundation of all that is good, the ground of our being. So when the mysteries are close at hand—and the miracles, whether you believe in god or not—you know you have a grounded religion, ready for the telling.

The End Is Near

The end is near. At least that's the talk among end-time fundamentalists. What with the best-selling *Left Behind* series of books and talk of the rapture on the Internet, religious liberals, once again, are out of the loop.

If I were focused on popularity, I, too, might dwell more on endings. Maybe not the Big Ending, but the little ones: the end of summer, love relationships gone by, friendships ebbing away, paychecks stopped, or good health or home life declining to nothing. Ended. Surely we do live with endings and loss and certain death, and were I the minister at another kind of church, I might make "endings" my focus. But that's not our way as Unitarian Universalists.

We are known as optimists. We are the people who say, *this* life, being alive right now, has value. The beginnings are the thing, not the endings. Armageddon is not the crowning glory for us. Heaven's a little unreliable in our view, and death is no reward. Other religions can have their endings, their prophecies, their rapture, their Apocalypse; we're in it for the present tense. We're going to cast our vote for life, capital "L" life, right here and now.

So then. What sense does it make to title a Unitarian Universalist column "The End Is Near"? It all hinges on this small reality: the word *end* has two meanings. The first, of course, is "the end, it's over, *finis*." But think about the second meaning, the word end as "meaning," or "goal," or "purpose," the way we use it in the phrase "the means to an end," or in the case of the *Oxford English Dictionary*'s example, "to eat and sleep supinely is the end [the goal, the purpose] of human blessing." Or the famous quote by one of Unitarianism's founders, William Ellery Channing, who said, "The great end in religious instruction is not to stamp our minds upon the young, but to stir up their own." Now that's the kind of end Unitarian Universalists can relate to.

We choose our "great end." As Unitarian Universalists, we take the bull by the horns and create meaning for ourselves, and purpose. The psychiatrist Viktor Frankl, who died over a decade ago, made this very point his claim to fame. Trying to cope with life in the concentration camps, Frankl, as many of you remember, came to the conclusion that above all, one must create meaning in life, no matter how dismal the circumstances. His most famous book, *Man's Search for Meaning*, is still in print in twenty-six languages.

We each have the chance to create meaning for ourselves, in some small way, right now. The ends, we hope, are near. What do we want our lives to look like? What's important? Maybe we plant bulbs for beauty down the road. Maybe this is the season to re-establish regular ties with relatives or, on the other hand, to sever those connections that are destructive. It might be the time to take ballroom dancing lessons, or take on the local manifestations of the Religious Right, or help out with the textile drive. Maybe this is the month to create the wise and

wacky website, or to take a quiet bath once a week without fail for a little re-grouping, or finally to join the Peace
Corps. We create meaningful lives, or if not meaningful
lives, then meaningful moments. We choose. That is our
way as Unitarian Universalists. We draw the ends near.

But creating meaning, choosing the courses of our
lives, is not the whole story of Unitarian Universalism.
To construct a purposeful life, a liberal religious life, a
life of great ends, encompasses more than a to-do list of
meaningful acts and spiritual disciplines.

We have hearts, too. We have human spirits, and as
religious people, we tend those spirits. Those ends are
near, too. You could call it your matter of perspective, an
attitude, an approach. Your way of being in the world,
your way of the spirit.

Astonishment is one such way, explained by my friend
and colleague Rev. Mark Belletini. He says,

Astonishment has been my daily portion since
long before I began to write. I am always astonished. If I am happy, I am astonished that I am
happy. If I am depressed, I am astonished that I am
depressed. If I am suspended between bliss and
dullness, I am astonished to be suspended. If I see
a liquid ambar tree in the fall, hear a mockingbird
in the spring, make love on a summer night, cry
in inconsolable grief in the midst of winter, I am
astonished. Whence those tears, whence the love
and the pleasure, the ears that hear, the thousand

tiny cones in the eye? I am astonished to be here at all, here on this earth at the edge of the abyss.

Astonishment is Mark's way. Yours may be gratitude, or joy, or perplexity, or "what good luck!" or fondness. Not so much that we're always in that mode, but we hold an awareness of a great spiritual end in the general neighborhood.

I've always heard it said that "end is near" talk is for other peoples' religions. Not so fast. Unitarian Universalists have ends in sight too, purposeful ends, ends that are worthy and just, ends that lift us up. And, I hope, those ends are near.

Hold on to Your Hats:
All of Unitarian Universalist History
in Just Under Two Thousand Words

Well folks, here we are, Unitarian Universalists who, on occasion, are called upon to explain ourselves. Our uncle asks about the new-fangled questionable religion we've stumbled into—he's never heard of it before—and it sounds a little sketchy to him. The guy across the hall thinks we've joined a cult that someone dreamed up ten minutes ago. The mom of our child's friend wants to be supportive—or maybe just tolerant—but not supportive enough to recognize a religion that has no grounding in history—that's her impression, anyway.

Maybe notes about our history will help. These could, of course, be sliced and diced in any number of ways. Certainly I would like to have included more continents, more diversity, more nuance, indeed, more technical accuracy. I especially would like to have included information about those countless courageous founders whose names and contributions are lost to us. But still, the history that follows might help with that uncle of yours.

Our particular history features generations and generations of people who seem first to lose their religion, and then, by means of private struggle and personal risk, find new ways of being religious. Our founders were doubters, thinkers, people for whom integrity counted for something. Through processes of theological reinterpretation and revolution, they found ways to continue their religious lives.

Our first notable ancestor was an Alexandrian named Origen. It was the early Third Century, when Christians were persecuted. Origen, at age seventeen, his father imprisoned and then killed as a Christian, was willing to accept martyrdom himself for his religious faith. But his mother thwarted his plan of leaving home and risking his life by hiding all his clothes. Origen went on to become a dedicated scholar, devoting himself single-mindedly to the pursuit of Christian truth through the use of reason. The more he studied the Bible, the more he began to doubt the usual notion of the existence of heaven and hell. Origen believed that everyone, not just Christians, not just "good" people, would find redemption. It was the "ultimate reconciliation of all souls with God," it was "universal salvation," it was "universalism." Origen's writings were eventually condemned as heresy, but Universalism lived on as a thread in our liberal history.

Another Alexandrian, a century later, was the first to champion the simplicity of God and the humanity of Jesus: Arius. The creed recited in many Christian churches today affirming Trinitarian doctrine and Christology was created to counteract the teachings of Arius!

And then there was Pelagius, the fourth-century English monk. At a time when Augustine insisted on the total depravity of human nature, Pelagius, bless him, courageously advocated moral free will and spiritual liberty. Pelagius was well-respected at the time, and while Augustine clearly had the upper hand, Pelagius posed a real threat to the Church's doctrine of innate corruption. Augustine won the debate. But again, a thread of faith has persisted: we have the ability to choose good over evil. We have Pelagius to thank for that theological position.

A big jump now to the Reformation, where our hero is a Spaniard named Michael Servetus. I have mixed feelings about Servetus. Here we have a nineteen-year-old kid who takes on both the Catholic and Protestant authorities. They believe in the Trinity; and Servetus says, and I quote, "Your Trinity is a product of subtlety and madness. The Gospel knows nothing of it." He was brilliant and intemperate. He infuriated the Inquisitors as well as Calvin. They gave him chance after chance to moderate his views, but he insulted them repeatedly, until, finally, Calvin had Servetus burned at the stake. Personally, I wish Servetus had seen fit to proceed with a little more caution and save himself. He did clearly prove there is no Trinity taught in the Bible, and that was important for a new theology. But I wonder, had he lived, where his theology would have taken him—and us.

Now to Poland and Transylvania, the cradle of European Unitarianism. Sixteenth century. Faustus Socinus. Socinus was the trusted theologian in a group of non-Trinitarian liberal congregations in Poland devoted to religious liberty, reason, and tolerance. The movement spread rapidly, attracting many of the most enlightened and gifted minds of that age. But they were persecuted—the "Socinian heresy" was stomped on, and Socinus himself was attacked in the streets of Krakow, his mouth filled with mud and his face smeared. Eventually, broken by the attacks, he died. Meanwhile, over in Transylvania, having adopted the Unitarian views of his court preacher, Ferenc Dávid (Francis David), the Unitarian king John Sigismund declared the first edict of religious toleration in 1568. You've heard the phrase, "We need not think alike to love alike"? That was Ferenc Dávid. In Transylvania, liberal congregations survived and continue to survive over four hundred years later as Unitarian churches.

England. Eighteenth Century. Religious liberals here knew about Socinianism: they advocated Socinian tolerance of differences in belief, they applied the Socinian test of reason to religious doctrines, and preached the Socinian concept that Jesus was simply a man. Here we come upon Joseph Priestley, discoverer of oxygen, Unitarian minister, and espouser of a number of liberal and unpopular causes, including the French Revolution. Priestley gave intellectual brilliance to the development of Unitarian religion and stimulated a mushrooming of Unitarian institutions. But established church leaders became exasperated, and they inflamed a mob. Priestley's home, laboratory, library, and Unitarian chapel were attacked and burned. He escaped by the skin of his teeth and, tempted by an invitation from his friend Thomas Jefferson, sailed to the United States in 1794, bringing his Unitarianism with him.

John Murray. The late 1700s. Another Englishman, a Universalist. Murray's life in England had begun to fall apart. His only child died, and then his wife, followed by his three sisters and his mother. He lost his job and landed in debtor's prison. When he got out, he resolved to go to America to seek a new life. John Murray did just that, and wound up on a ship that was eventually grounded on a sandbar off the coast of New Jersey. While the ship's crew waited for a fair wind and a high tide to move them along, Murray went ashore, where he met a farmer—Thomas Potter. It so happens that this Thomas Potter had built a chapel nearby, and was just waiting for a preacher who believed in universal salvation to appear on the scene. Potter became convinced that God had sent John Murray to preach in his chapel. Murray, however, was not at all convinced. Potter said, "The wind will never change, sir, until you preach for us." And Murray's ship remained stuck until Sunday, when Murray began his preaching career, bringing Universalism to the colonies.

Universalism was a religion that praised God and preached a loving theology of inclusivity in heaven and also here on earth. Therefore, Universalists devoted themselves to prison reform, building schools, temperance, pacifism, and women's rights (ordaining Olympia Brown to the Universalist ministry in 1863).

We now have Unitarianism and Universalism on the American continent. It is the early nineteenth century, and Calvinist orthodoxy, straight from the Puritans, is the status quo. Universalists, with their universal salvation, offered relief from the Calvinist notion of damnation. Hosea Ballou became the Universalists' greatest leader through his public speaking and publications, spreading the seeds that Murray had sown.

Unitarian-oriented clergy began more and more to sit up and take notice of Calvinistic pessimism about human nature. The prevailing theology in the culture forced religious liberals to come to grips with their own theologies of human free will, dignity, and rationality. William Ellery Channing confirmed the presence of the new theological movement, and rallied the liberals together as a theological group. By the third decade of the nineteenth century, many of the Puritan Congregational churches began to call themselves Unitarian.

Every generation of American Unitarians has questioned the religion they inherited. Almost as soon as American Unitarianism was established, a young generation of Transcendentalists—Ralph Waldo Emerson and Theodore Parker among them—changed the liberal religious orientation from one of empiricism and historicism to a religion of direct intuition. Unitarianism drifted away from belief in biblical revelation and the sole inspiration of Jesus.

The Universalists did retain the Christian basis of their faith more completely. But they, too, changed over the years, and by the early decades of the twentieth century, Universalism emphasized the notion that evil is the result of "unjust social and economic conditions." Universalism, according to reformer Clarence Skinner, was economic and social as well as spiritual.

The generations continued, and our religion continued to evolve. The rise of the humanist movement among the Unitarians was an attempt to reformulate liberal theology on non-theistic grounds. Universalists moved from their long-standing emphasis on universal salvation to an understanding of Universalism as universal religion— "boundless in scope, as broad as humanity, as infinite as the universe."

By mid-century, the leadership of both Unitarianism and Universalism recognized the advantages of combining efforts through consolidation. The proposed merger was controversial for both Unitarians and Universalists, each quite naturally fearing a loss of tradition and identity. But finally, in 1961, the plan was overwhelmingly ratified by the individual congregations and then by the American Unitarian Association Annual Meeting and the Universalist General Assembly.

Generation after generation, Unitarian Universalists continue to examine the religion, reshape it, persist in it, and find joy in it. Frederick May Eliot, president of the American Unitarian Association from 1937 to 1958, said, "one of the most interesting aspects of our history is the process by which the radicals of one generation have come to be regarded as '100 percent Unitarians' by succeeding generations. The truth of the matter is that we are a church in which growth is not only permitted but encouraged—growth in thought, growth in sensitiveness to moral values, growth in courage to put religion to work in the world."

My colleague Rev. Jack Mendelsohn offers us this benediction (adapted):

We have inherited quite a religion.

It is lived. It is not just a set of bromides and pietisms. It is a serious effort to conduct life according to principles and ideals.

It is emotional, heart-swelling. It is even naïve. In spite of uncertainty, it does not rule out leaps of faith.

It is free, not bound by tradition, inheritance, geography, nor the passing parade.

It is first-hand, a personal experience.

It is responsible. It does not try to escape the consequences of decision.

It is growing. It never thinks of itself as perfected and final. It embraces humility, recognizing that faith is not certainty where there is in fact mystery.

It is compassionate. It understands that religions universally wrap their essence in myth. It reaches to grasp and appreciate the truths bound up in the myths of other believers.

It is tough on its possessors, committing them to sacrifice, but it is tender toward those who disagree.

It is social, struggling to realize its own vision at community, national, and world levels.

It is radiant, blessing its possessor with courage, serenity, and zest.

This is our history, and also our hope.

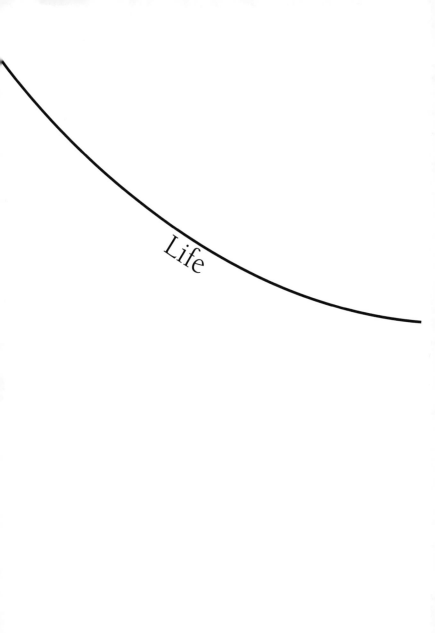

The Marker's Meaning

Some years back I read a story in the *Indianapolis Star*. It was a Sunday paper kind of an article about finding happiness. "The truth is," says the column, "the real secret to happiness isn't a secret at all. It's just not that pleasant a truth. Nor does it rhyme. Which is why it is never cross-stitched, hung over the fireplace or emblazoned on tote bags. The secret to happiness is realizing that life is often hard."

A local colleague, Wendy Bell, used to talk about riding the bus on her commute through a suburb called Arlington Heights. You have to remember that even suburbs are very old in the Boston area, by American standards at least, and Wendy would sit there on the bus and watch out the window until she saw it. She would sit there on the bus and sooner or later there it would be, the monument—the stone marker—the one that tells the account of one day in the life of Samuel Whittemore.

"On April 19th, 1775," the marker reads, "Samuel Whittemore was shot, bayoneted, beaten, and left for dead." He was eighty years old. Dr. Tufts, of Medford, declared that it was useless to dress Mr. Whittemore's wounds.

Each of us has some pretty tough days. And it's not always the big-time tough stuff like literally being left for dead that gets us—it's the lost sock that can just as easily put us over the edge, or running out of cat food, or remembering to save that all-important computer file just as the screen goes blank. But whatever it is, whether your child won't sleep through the night or your feelings for your partner are clearly waning, whatever it is . . . at least you are not Samuel Whittemore on his "no good very bad day." Thus far, no matter how bad it feels, you have not *actually* been shot, bayoneted, beaten and left for dead.

For some of us, salvation comes, historically at least, in "salvation by character." We believe there is something wonderful inside us—you could call it inherent dignity and worth—that allows us to work toward good character, wholeness, healing, and all that is good. We have within us a little core of natural hope—some bit of life that lies waiting to spring into action. And even better, we don't have to just sit and wait: we can act to realize that hope, that life, that wholeness. In spite of the difficulties in our own experience and of life in the larger world, we do what we can. Therein lies our salvation.

Rabbi Harold Schulweis writes in "Playing with Three Strings," a poem about Yitzhak Perlman,

> On one occasion one of his violin strings broke.
> > The audience grew silent,
> > the violinist did not leave the stage.
> Signaling the maestro,
> > The violinist played with power and intensity
> > > on only three strings.

With three strings, he modulated, changed, and
    Recomposed the piece in his head . . .

The audience screamed delight,
    Applauded their appreciation.
Asked how he had accomplished this feat,
    The violinist answered
It is my task to make music with what remains. . . .

That hope, that strength, that "salvation by character," is what many of us have been looking for. We have found that people have a light inside. We have a spirit. We bounce back. Maybe politically, maybe spiritually or psychologically, or medically, or morally. Sometimes in small ways—you got up and wrote a pretty decent letter to your local newspaper this morning, even though your coffeemaker let you down, or you ran an extra mile along the river. You can feel some hope inside, a little glow inside, hope for the world and for us all. Your power and your zest come back—you can feel it in your fingers and toes, you can imagine a time when lessons will have been learned—a few lessons anyway—a time when your efforts and our efforts together will pay off and no one— no one—is ever left for dead.

Which reminds me. Samuel Whittemore's marker. Eighty years old in 1775—shot, bayoneted, beaten, and left for dead in Arlington. Samuel Whittemore survived that day. More than survived. He recovered and lived to be ninety-eight years old.

Life, the world, it can all get pretty desperate—shot, bayoneted, beaten, and left for dead. But we believe in the light of life, in that something inside that can awaken and shine and sing all songs of hope.

Let's Go Ride the Rides

Last weekend at Spartanburg's Spring Fling, I was paying attention to 90-degree heat and shoving crowds, standing in line at the bumper-car ride with my two boys. One of them kept changing his mind about whether he wanted to ride. What he really wanted to do was toss rubber chickens into a pot, five tries for two dollars. My brain was a rubber chicken. I had just dragged the children all over the fair looking for the writers with whom I was supposed to sign books and the folks from my church with whom I was supposed to sell beer. I couldn't find either group, and the whole time I was looking for those people, both boys were pulling on me asking, "Can we ride the rides now?" Sigh. So I said, "Let's go ride the rides." Here we were in line, and into my head came this thought: "I am in hell."

When I saw my older son dive into a car and start manhandling the wheel, waiting for the ride to start, I moved into the shade with his brother to watch. There my brain cooled off enough to remember to enjoy my life, to be there for the beauty and grace in that situation. I saw my son's mouth open wide with joy, its inside stained red by tiger's-blood-flavored shaved ice. He was in a state of bliss, being slammed from behind and from all sides by other bumper-car drivers. He threw back his head and laughed, putting the pedal to the metal in reverse, snapping his head forward as he took aim, and slammed into another car, looking sideways at the other driver, grinning, not quite able to believe this was actually *allowed. Jubilee. Bubbles of joy changed my breathing. I was having fun. Here was beauty, and here was grace, and here I was in the middle of it.*

— Meg Barnhouse, "Trying to Be There"

So Meg is at Spartanburg's big carnival, and it's hot, and she has promises to keep, her kids are pestering her for the chance to toss rubber chickens and get over to the bumper cars, and to her everlasting credit, what does she say? She says—in a moment of prize-winning good parenting—she says, "Let's go ride the rides."

And here's what she does not say: She does not say, "The lines are too long, the place is a madhouse, there's too much going on at once, and I'm way too hot and tired." She does not actually say, "Truly and certainly, I am burning in hell." What Meg does say is, "Let's go ride the rides."

Ever been to a place where it's hot and muggy outside, and there are lots of eager people gathered everywhere? Ever been to a place where there are too many things going on at once and the lines are long and you get hot and tired? A place, maybe, where however fun it had seemed like it would be when you thought up the idea of going, there later come moments when you wonder what in the world you were thinking? And then, and then, you snap out of it and you cool off your brain enough to re-jigger your attitude and your attention, and something healthy and spiritual and calm kicks in and at last you say to yourself, "Let's go ride the rides!" The dimness of your soul passes, and you are up and running toward the beauty, toward the joy.

Unitarian Universalists ride the rides. We believe that everybody is invited, and not only invited, but free to choose among the death-defying scary rides, the tame little whirling tea cup rides, the classic merry-go-round, the rides in the dark, the sentimental rides that have scenery and cheerful songs, or, yes, the bumper cars. We have a theology that requires us to decide for ourselves what kind of a person we want to be, what kind of ride we want to take given the constraints on our lives, and once that's all decided, we are required to help the rest of the folks climb into their seats. Only when we've done that does our religion, our unfettered religion, encourage us to find the beauty and the joy.

Unitarian Universalism encourages us to ride the rides with heartfelt joy at the beauty of it all—not every religion pushes that. We can sing if we want to as we go round and round, or shriek with delight. Ooh and ahh at the view from the top, take delight in our companions, or enjoy the weightlessness or up-side-downedness of whatever ride we signed up for. But whether your ride is bumpy or smooth, daring or comforting, the joy of the experience is yours for the taking.

But wait. Life's no amusement park. We all know that. We bring joy and beauty into our focus in the context of pain and confusion writ small and large. Disaster, grief, deep disappointment, betrayal, divine discontent and the hungry heart, injustice—in our own lives and across the globe. And yet, and yet, the potential for the good in life always exists. The perfect three-pointer exacted by the correct basketball team, the hurricane blowing out to sea just in time, kindness in the face of crisis when the waters rise high, the grand and glorious symphony. Things of beauty, occasions of joy, everywhere you look. They calm us down, slow the gallop, remind us of the peace we're breathing in and the love we're breathing out.

We all get to have "spots of time." Not the fleeting happy moments that flow through our lives, but rather the far deeper, poignant spiritual moments that continue to resonate with meaning many years later. These are, to my mind, the religious moments, that offer us renovation, nourishment, and the healthy repair, even when experienced watching the bumper cars at the Spartanburg Spring Fling.

We each get to have the beauty and the joy. We turn our attention and there it is. Presto, we find ourselves in a spiritual moment; abracadabra, we are changed.

Calm Soul of All Things

"The Frost performs its secret ministry," writes Samuel Taylor Coleridge, in his poem "The Frost at Midnight."

It's 1797 in the hilly southwest of England, near the coast—Devonshire. Coleridge is sitting in his house by the fire on a winter night at midnight. His first baby—Hartley is his name—is asleep right there. Maybe Coleridge is up late because of the baby—who knows. Coleridge's wife, Sara, is probably asleep, which is something of a blessing, as we're told she was a bit of a nag in the eyes of her philosopher-poet husband.

> The Frost performs its secret ministry,
> Unhelp'd by any wind. The owlet's cry
> Came loud—and hark, again! loud as before.
> The inmates of my cottage, all at rest,
> Have left me to that solitude, which suits
> Abstruser musings: save that at my side
> My cradled infant slumbers peacefully.
> 'Tis calm indeed! so calm, that it disturbs
> And vexes meditation with its strange
> And extreme silentness. Sea, hill, and wood,
> This populous village! Sea, and hill, and wood,
> With all the numberless goings on of life,
> Inaudible as dreams! . . .

So Coleridge (I call him Coleridge because he hated

the name Samuel) is startled by the calm. He is taken with the "extreme silentness." Daily life has become as "inaudible as dreams." He is at peace.

For some of you, this scene is your idea of heaven. You recognize this feeling of deep peace as a dream come true. You know the quiet to be spiritually satisfying. To be silent. To feel the solitude. To know the stillness of winter. Peace.

Of course, just as many of you think Coleridge and anyone like him is nuts. Who cares if it's 1797—you want the TV on for a little background noise. You wonder if any of the neighbors are still awake—maybe they feel like playing cards. Or the baby's cradle needs fixing, that's right, and it's never too late to get a start on the laundry. This "solitude" routine sounds lonely and boring. *Silence* means nothing's happening! *Solitude* means nobody's come by to visit. *Stillness* means nothing's getting done.

Occasionally, I write a sermon that highlights the solitary life of the spirit, and people ask when I'll write a sermon about "our religion." Just as often, in response to a sermon about the importance of community or social justice, people will ask the same question: "When will you be writing about our religion?"

Of course for us Unitarian Universalists, it's all religion. As individuals we may emphasize different aspects— some of us are looking for spiritual peace; some of us crave the comfort and excitement of religious community (online or in person) and purposeful action—but it's all religion.

Whether we're the people looking for deep silence or committed action and community, we have equal access to the internal stillness that can serve each one of us well. Ira Progoff, in *The Well and the Cathedral*, suggests a metaphor. We can imagine spirituality, he says, as a single straight shaft which plunges like a well far into the earth. And there, deep within, each of us can find an underground stream that nourishes, awakens, and renews us. This stream is a power that moves along beneath the entire world. He goes on to say that all kinds of people representing all of the religions of the world tap this same underground stream; religions are simply cathedrals built over these wells, places that mark the spots where people have encountered the underground stream and returned inspired.

When we experience the awe of the winter seacoast, the birth of a child, the compassion of a friend, or a connection with the universe, we are drawing on this underground stream. When we ask ultimate questions we are drawing on this underground stream. When we mourn or when we celebrate our good fortune we are drawing on this underground stream.

This sense of peace, this stream of religious nurture, is available to each of us in a form appropriate to our personalities and theologies and stages in life. Perhaps you are up early, you bundle up, and take a February walk in the woods. Maybe you putter in your workshop on a balmy Saturday and find your renewal there. Or you put some music on and take a long, hot bath. Or you are a parent of young children, and you wait for that instant between the time the children go to sleep and the time you fall into bed, when you can find five minutes to read the paper, and you feel the better for it. Perhaps you live alone and on these dark evenings you light a candle, taking the time to remember people you've loved who have long since died. Maybe you are Coleridge, by the fire, late on a very cold night, feeling the "frost performing its secret ministry."

The winter stillness, the underground stream, the calm soul of all things, is always out there and available, "inaudible as dreams."

Golfing with Monkeys

According to Gregory Knox Jones in Play the Ball Where the Monkey Drops It, *when the British colonized India, they also indulged themselves in building golf courses. Apparently the golf course in Calcutta was built near a monkey habitat, and that location created a problem the builders had not foreseen. The monkeys took to the game of golf, as they understood it, and thoroughly relished chasing the little white balls. Once in possession of the ball, they seemed to enjoy throwing it somewhere else.*

The keepers of the golf course tried fencing the monkeys out, but no fence ever built could hold them. They attempted to lure the monkeys away, but the monkeys could think of nothing more fascinating than chasing golf balls and being chased by golfers.

The golfers finally found they had no other choice but to include the monkeys in new rules of the game. The new rule was if a monkey picked up your ball, you must play the ball where the monkey finally dropped it. This could work several ways. You might hit a drive screaming straight down the fairway only to have a monkey toss it into the rough. But, it is equally possible that you might slice the ball onto a wrong fairway only to have a monkey retrieve it and place it on the proper green. The monkeys brought equal measures of gratuitous bad and good luck to the game.

Life is a little bit like this. You can work hard and live right, or play all of the angles that you figure will lead "to success," and some monkey will drop your ball onto the wrong fairway. On the other hand, many of us have been saved from a host of dumb mistakes by similarly random good luck. Play the ball where the monkey drops it? It is a view that encourages us to take the tough breaks that come along less as a personal affront and more as an opportunity to make the best of a life that never will be completely predictable. What better choice is there?

—Rev. John Nichols, church newsletter

Personal theology is important. Years ago, we used to call it religion: "Your religion is important," we'd say. Then society morphed a bit, and the popular word became *spirituality*. Now it seems that the word *spirituality* is giving way to the word *theology*.

Those who care about etymology will be bothered that in popular parlance, *religion*, *spirituality*, and *theology* seem bound together in one synonymous lump, when technically their meanings are distinct. But there's no help for it. Out there in the world, matters of religion are squishy, and most folks don't bother with precision.

Whatever we're calling it, it's vital. And vibrant. Fundamental to our well-being. Whether you focus on a god or goddess who holds you, a human role model who inspires you, a natural world that includes you, a spirit that enlivens you, a universe that feels capricious in its randomness, or any other religious perspective, your approach to living will depend on it.

As Unitarian Universalists, we haven't committed to a

permanent creed. We won't get thrown out of church if our beliefs change, and moments both of confusion and clarity are par for the course. We are free to experiment with all kinds of religious metaphors, stories and images when describing the human experience, and we develop our own responses. This is where golfing with monkeys comes in.

Though we need to acknowledge the offensive aspects of colonial rule, the monkey scenario illustrates just such human experience. Whoever you are, however you understand the image theologically, spiritually, or religiously, and whatever you think the monkeys represent, those monkeys will move your golf ball a time or two, for good and for ill, and you will need to come to terms with it.

In an interview, I heard Alan Ball, the creator of the TV show "Six Feet Under," use the term *lyric existentialism*. This is an unlikely phrase, but whatever it's intended to mean, I'm pretty sure it includes monkeys on the golf course. Lyric existentialism has got to convey a light approach to life from wherever you have to play the golf ball. It must have something to say about capriciousness in the world, and finding the get-up-and-go to drive the ball home. Surely it accepts the positives and negatives of the human predicament.

Playing golf with monkeys. For me it's lyric existentialism. For you it might be a cosmic plan unfolding, or something about God's will. Whatever your response, it will be religious. Or spiritual. Or theological.

When We Feel Transformed

Most days are ordinary days, and I go about my business. I run into a former intern, and he tells me about a deeply moving lecture he attended. I get a phone call, and the person on the other end of the line talks about lunch at a Japanese noodle shop, and how her conversation at the table had been transformational. A colleague feels profoundly changed by the fact of an enterprising squirrel in a busy section of the city.

I begin to feel jaded, as though brushing my teeth is supposed to be deeply moving, and crossing the street transformational. I begin to wonder what ever happened to capital "T" Transformation, where lives are changed and spirits are truly renewed for the long haul.

But then again, I know that nobody preaches the message of the wonder of small things more than I do: to see majesty in the ordinary; to find meaning in the every day. In the words of William Blake,

> To see a World in a grain of sand,
> And a Heaven in a wild flower,
> Hold Infinity in the palm of your hand,
> And Eternity in an hour.

That's what I preach: everyday transformation.

So I got to thinking about how maybe I talk too much about the importance of day-to-day perspective, at the expense of deeper transformation. Sometimes we change our lives not only by noticing the grains of sand and the wild flowers, but also by taking charge of our lives in big, huge ways. We decide we want to try to give birth or adopt children, or we make the decision to move into an assisted-living complex, or we pack our bags and join the Peace Corps, or in the midst of an errand, we simply stop by the desert's edge until clarity appears about giving up the driver's license, training as a Web designer, or abandoning professional tennis and giving belly-dancing a serious try. We decide, we choose, we act. We jump-start the process of life's transformation.

Sometimes, of course, we are just living our lives, and an unpredictable circumstance arises—serious illness, for example—and we decide to make the best use we can of that circumstance. We hadn't been out there looking for deeply meaningful experiences or transformation, but the occasion arose, and we could either knuckle under or adopt a positive perspective. Somehow we had the spunk to transform our outlook and gain from the experience.

So it was with the columnist and author Anna Quindlen, who wrote in *Thinking Out Loud*,

It was very cold the night my mother died. She was a little older than I am today, a young woman with five young children who had been eaten alive by disease, had wasted away to a wisp, had turned into a handful of bones wound round with pale silk. . . . It was not until the aftermath of my mother's death that I began to realize that I would have to fashion a life for myself—and that is what I have been trying to do, in a workmanlike way, ever since. This seems rather ordinary to me now, but at the beginning it was odd and frightening. Up until that point life had fashioned me. There had been almost no decisions for me to make, in part because I was not permitted to make them, and in part because I saw no path other than the one I was on. . . . And then a kind of earthquake in the center of my life shook everything up, and left me to rearrange the pieces.

Part of what we do as religious people is rearrange the pieces after an earthquake shakes everything up. And part of what we do is ask ourselves during ordinary times if it's time to initiate a transformational experience. In her poem, "Now I Become Myself," May Sarton says,

Now I become myself. It's taken
Time, many years and places;
I have been dissolved and shaken,
Worn other people's faces,
Run madly, as if Time were there,
Terribly old, crying a warning,
"Hurry, you will be dead before—"
(What? Before you reach the morning?
Or the end of the poem is clear?
Or love safe in the walled city?)

Now to stand still, to be here,
Feel my own weight and density! . . .
All fuses now, falls into place
From wish to action, word to silence,
My work, my love, my time, my face
Gathered into one intense
Gesture of growing like a plant. . . .

That's what we do as Unitarian Universalists, we fuse and fall into place. We face the big transformational issues, take a hand in fashioning our lives, and, with luck, we come out ahead. May our spirits be strong for the task, and may we feel grateful for the chance.

The Dim Soul and What to Do About It

On the phone the other day, talking with a colleague about some small denominational matter, I could hear her toddler in the background, and her newborn baby. And the doorbell and the dog barking at the doorbell and her dryer signaling that if she wanted to avoid wrinkles, she'd best get her clothes out immediately and fold them. When I asked my friend how things were going, she said, "Actually, they're a little hectic—I'm going to New York tomorrow to lead a four-day retreat." "Oh—on what?" I asked. "On 'Living the Balanced Spiritual Life,'" she said, and then she added, "Isn't that the joke of the century?"

The pressure is on. The pressure is on to take the pressure off. Racing around, feeling overwhelmed and stretched, the plate too full, the day too short—all of that has gone completely out of style. Those inclined to brag talk of calm hours of meditation and massage; the folks who work overtime feel a little sheepish.

Times change. Horatio Alger, my father's hero (whom he knew only as the "rags to riches" dime novelist), would be laughed out of the spirituality group today—so would my dad, for that matter. The point at that time was hard work, courage, and determination. Dad would have been puzzled by people striking an early morning Yoga pose, seeking a balanced life.

Maybe you fall somewhere between the committed spiritual seeker and the frantic hard worker. You'll be happy if you can eat a little healthier and listen to more of the music that you love. Get the birdhouse up and see who appears. Make it over to the lake before the bugs set in at dusk. Write letters in longhand, climb the mountain in record time, repair the cuckoo clock—concentrating with all intensity on the tiny mechanical parts. But then again, not all of us need to slow down; some of us need to move faster and get a few things done. Others of us do need the discipline of a daily practice to keep us grounded and breathing easy. Some of us want to call this kind of focus "spirituality"; some of us don't.

In any case, it seems to me that each one of us understands what the nineteenth-century hymn-writer George Croly meant when he wrote,

> I ask no dream, no prophet ecstasies,
>   No sudden rending of the veil of clay;
> No angel visitant, no opening skies;—
>   But take the dimness of my soul away.

Croly is willing to settle. Sure, wouldn't it be grand to know a perfect peace, to embrace a life that never gets out of hand, to check in on a regular basis with, as Croly puts it, the angels? In this instance, I vote with Croly for the smaller scale. Wouldn't simple zest for life, its loves and loveliness, unfettered by dull fatigue or inattention, be a great gift indeed? As Garrison Keillor describes it, "Left to our own devices, we Woebegonians go straight for the small potatoes. Majestic doesn't appeal to us; we like the Grand Canyon better with Clarence and Arlene parked in front of it, smiling." For many of us, it doesn't get better than that, and we don't really need it to.

Croly yearns to enliven the dim, unbalanced soul. How is it that on a particular day during an average hour you are struck dumb by one of life's wonders? What is that? Surely there's a recipe, a series of steps, a chant or something! And actually, there may be. Popular books, magazines, websites, religious publications—suggestions are available for the asking—and every one of them works for somebody. Gratitude returns, and perspective, and we are lighter on our feet.

Universalist minister Max Kapp wrote in his poem "Gratitude,"

> Often I have felt that I must praise my world
> For what my eyes have seen these many years,
> And what my heart has loved.
> And often I have tried to start my lines:
>> "Dear Earth," I say,
>> And then I pause
>> To look once more.
>> Soon I am bemused
>> And far away in wonder.
> So I never get beyond "Dear Earth."

Unitarian Universalists run the gamut. From Clarence and Arlene in front of the Grand Canyon to "Dear Earth" . . . and the subsequent spiritual drift. Our souls brighten in so many contexts and in so many manifestations that it's a minister's folly to drill down very deep into strategic detail. Heaven knows that lots of folks are more or less content with the equilibrium they've found in life. But still.

If you are casting about for the balance we hear so much about, the spiffing up of a dim soul, try focusing on some of the time-tested classics: Gratitude. Love. Perspective. Attention. Meditate on them, pray, or think them over. Put them into play; embody them, dance them. Google for them and see if you find anything you like. Make yourself some promises or add reflections to your blog. Breathe them in and out. Brighten up your soul.

Bad Information

Surrounded by people whose language I couldn't understand, who didn't look like me, who were stranded, agitated, and hungry, I guarded my hard-boiled eggs. Instinctively. Before I had a chance to think about it. And I don't even like eggs!

I am, I like to believe, a generous person, or at least a person who has manners. I enjoy interacting with people I don't know, even when communication seems difficult, and these hours in a rural Chinese airport should have fit the bill. Traveling beyond my own element feels enlivening and like a generally good thing. I don't mind the uncertainty of erratic or mysterious meals. So what was the big deal about hard-boiled eggs?

In his poem, "One Source of Bad Information," Robert Bly explains,

> There's a boy in you about three
> Years old who hasn't learned a thing for thirty
> Thousand years. Sometimes it's a girl.
>
> This child has to make up its mind
> How to save you from death. He says things like:
> "Stay home. Avoid elevators. Eat only elk."
>
> You live with this child but you don't know it.
> You're in the office, yes, but live with this boy
> At night. He's uninformed, but he does want

To save your life. And he has. Because of this boy
You survived a lot. He's got six big ideas.
Five don't work. Right now he's repeating them
    to you.

I have—we all have—30,000-year-old safety tips bouncing between our ears. "Alert! You don't know when you'll eat next, you're among an unknown tribe, and you have only three hard-boiled eggs! Conceal those eggs!"

Well, that's ridiculous advice for a traveler in a Chinese airport, even when the food stalls are closed and the flights are cancelled. Yes, the three-year-old is repeating six big ideas to me, five of them don't work, and this thing about the eggs is one of them.

There are others. We all have candidates we could put up for a vote.

One candidate, it seems to me, advocates security. Whether it's the "Red Menace" of the 1950s, genocidal polio vaccine, or Iraqi weapons of mass destruction, people all over the world hear internal voices, very old and very deep, that call for immediate methods of stomping out the trouble—hang the cost, the ramifications, the evidence, the human rights, the loss of life. "Trouble! They're coming to get us! Quick! Get your weapons!" I can hear echoes of that timeless dictum in my own head. How often is it one of the five that doesn't work?

Another candidate for big ideas that don't work surely lies in the area of gender identity and sexual practice. I live in Massachusetts, USA, where same-sex marriage is legal. Visitors from Kansas recently picketed schools and churches in my town bearing signs that said, "God hates fags." What 30,000-year-old big idea bumped around inside their heads?

How about consumption? The reluctance to deal with global warming? Here's the voice I hear, ancient and persistent: "Get the stuff you need. Get more than you need, just in case. Feather the nest. Grow your children big and smart. Cut down the last tree if you need to." I know that this is the voice of the antediluvian three-year-old girl valiantly trying to save my family and me from death. I know that her message lurks deep within me. And I know that she's spouting one of the five ideas that doesn't work.

You get my drift.

Unitarian Universalists commit to a search for truth and meaning, even as we struggle with whatever primordial imperatives we hear. And we are working toward social justice, in spite of any hard-wired, sketchy advice that's lingered for 30,000 years. For me, it's not always obvious, and certainly not always easy. There was, for example, that thing about the eggs.

When Things Don't Go from Bad to Worse

The snows had scarcely melted last June when 24-year-old Joama and her three male cousins, yak herders in the remote mountains of northern Tibet, embarked on the most sublime journey of their lives.

Their departure was not marked by any ceremony. "We just started out," she recalled. The four began mumbling mantras and raised their hands to heaven. They dropped to their knees and flung their bodies forward, fully prone against the damp earth. Then they stood up, took three small steps, and repeated the sequence.

For more than five months now they have prostrated themselves this way, all day every day, inch-worming their way to Lhasa and its holy sites. They slowly made their way through more than 100 miles of some of the world's harshest terrain, starting from above 14,000 feet, then followed a highway 200 more miles into Lhasa. . . .

"This has been our lifelong dream," said Joama, who spoke on the sidewalk as she paused for tea.

"We're doing this so our future can be better."

—Erik Eckholm, New York Times

Joama wants a better future. Who doesn't? Like so many of us, she believes that if she takes the right action, she can hedge her bets against upcoming misery.

Of course, what constitutes "right action" varies considerably: The Penobscot Indians say they are trying to build

139

a better future with nutritional programs that undermine drug and alcohol use. In England, the Children's Society works against poverty and social exclusion to build a better future. A group in Eritrea dreams of a better future based on an animal-feeding program that includes halophytes— plants that grow in salt water. New Zealand's retirement commissioner claims a better future can be had through financial planning ("and," she says, "maybe a little boogie boarding at Waihi Beach").

I work toward a better future myself—by recycling cardboard boxes, keeping my insurance policy up-to-date, paying my church pledge, voting for the good guys, flossing my teeth—that kind of thing. I hope it'll help.

But not until I saw the small groups of Tibetans who wore protective mitts or strapped protective blocks of wood to their hands, people rising and falling with every three footsteps, did I feel I'd really witnessed the driving power of human concern for the future. In the face of an existence where things so often don't go well, it is reasonable to respond with drastic action.

But is that what we all assume? That things won't go well? We get pretty busy preparing for the worst.

Here's the thing: Once in a while, the future works out just fine. It just does. Not because of the nutritional programs or the spiritual discipline, not because of the boogie boards or halophytes, and not because of all that cardboard tied with twine. Some would credit a benevolent universe, others would see the hand of God—I'd call it great good luck. I wish the language were inclusive, but a poem by a Welsh poet (who, these days, prefers not to be identified) puts it like this:

> Sometimes things don't go, after all,
> from bad to worse. Some years, muscadel
> faces down frost; green thrives; the crops don't fail,
> sometimes a man aims high, and all goes well.
>
> A people sometimes will step back from war;
> elect an honest man; decide they care
> enough, that they can't leave some stranger poor.
> Some men become what they were born for.
>
> Sometimes our best efforts do not go
> amiss; sometimes we do as we meant to.
> The sun will sometimes melt a field of sorrow
> that seemed hard frozen: may it happen for you.

A two-year-old Tibetan girl, wearing a pink hat, kept an eye on her mother as mom prostrated, walked three steps, prostrated again, mile after mile, day after day. For a few minutes, I watched the little girl as her mother worked so hard to build a better future. As the mother bent, kneeled, and lay flat, touching her calloused forehead to the ground, the girl and her hat skipped around her. Romping, really. She was just a little kid, and from the looks of her, she was completely clueless that things might go from bad to worse. Mom knew. But, as the poet says, "Sometimes things don't go, after all, from bad to worse." Just for the moment, I sided with the child.

Beyond What's for Lunch

I never saw the piano or the truck. Just the cliff.

George and Evelyn Frey built a guest lodge in the canyon in 1925. It's hard to imagine why they chose a spot on the floor of Frijoles Canyon, given that the only way down is a steep and narrow trail a mile and a half down from the canyon rim. Hardly a tourist thoroughfare.

As if the challenge of the remote location weren't enough, evidently running a guest lodge in the 1920s required (at least in the minds and hearts of George and Evelyn) a piano and a truck. So piece by piece they hauled a Dodge pickup down the little trail, and similarly, a piano.

George and Evelyn Frey, late of Bandelier, New Mexico, lived lives of industrious folly, human ambition, splendid success. That was their recipe for living life. What's yours?

Most of us think we know what life is—I know I do. It's what Garrison Keillor says it is: "tying shoe laces, flipping pancakes, starting cars, putting on your jacket now that it's getting to be the end of September." It's being born, and playing with LEGOs, watching cartoons on TV, doing algebra, eating fries, buying that first sofa, earning a paycheck, retiring in hopes of a little travel or peace and quiet—that's how it goes, doesn't it? Isn't that the recipe for living life, more or less?

No. That can't be it. A robot could do that stuff. There's got to be more to life, more to being human.

I checked out some resources, some guidelines for living life. One little book from the 1880s, entitled *Don't: A Manual of Mistakes & Improprieties More or Less Prevalent in Conduct and Speech*, keeps it pretty simple—just a few rules and you'll be human, or at least civilized, which at the time was about as good as it got. For example, "Don't use meaningless exclamations, such as 'Oh crackey!'" "Don't say gents for gentlemen, nor pants for pantaloons. These are inexcusable vulgarisms." "Don't sneer at people, or continually crack jokes at their expense." "Don't play the accordion, the violin, the piano, or any musical instrument, to excess. Your neighbors have nerves."

Follow those guidelines, and bingo—you're a splendid example of living life right.

After that little foray, I abandoned the research route, and simply got to thinking: what is it that we are looking for, beyond the neatly tied shoelaces and the retirement plan? Beyond driving the kids from basketball to bowling. Beyond what's for lunch?

One can imagine several answers—we want love, maybe, or security, or reliable good health. Maybe we long for the feeling of connection to a healthy family, or to a couple of close friends, or a wide and caring community. We may want to know the experience of getting up in the morning to a brand new day that looks like it's going to be fun, or we want to feel a sense of well-being deep inside, and self-respect, and satisfaction for a job well done and a life well-lived. We want to know that we've done our bit for social justice, paused to take in the quiet and the grandeur, that we've been alive, and good for something and grateful; that at the end of the day we will, as they say, have lived a good life.

Those are the kinds of things that when we've got them, we know we're not robots. It's the kind of list that, when taken all together, means a person is spiritual— that is to say, fully human.

I like to believe that most anybody who's in possession of the basics of food, shelter, and freedom can invent a satisfying recipe for life. A spiritual strategy. That's what Unitarian Universalists do, after all: we ponder, we observe, we notice our inner inclinations and rational strategies and measure them against the realities of the world. We experiment, take a few fliers, examine the ethics, connect with whatever gives us meaning. And we live our lives.

It would be convenient, I know, if ministers handed out the recipes for living full and satisfying lives once and for all. We don't, of course, but I can offer a couple of possible ingredients by way of example, which might just cook up a hearty, satisfying life. My recipe would include:

Know what your heaven looks like.

The travel writer Wade Davis remarks,

I once met in the Yukon an elderly Sekani man who was completely confounded by a missionary's notion of heaven. He couldn't believe anyone could be expected to give up smoking, drinking, swearing, carousing, and all the things that made life worth living in order to go to a place where they didn't allow animals. "No caribou?" he would say in complete astonishment.

He knew what heaven should look like.

I have begun to notice that people who know what heaven looks like are on to something. I watch for it now.

So in Montreal, on a day when it was thirty-eight degrees below zero Fahrenheit, in a drafty, unfinished warehouse loft in the old town—a very cool loft in every sense of the word—this is what I notice: a royal blue Hawaiian lap steel guitar, hockey skates, chop sticks, a huge pink piñata, two turntables for spinning, Vietnamese *sauce de poisson*, a tall and rickety wooden ladder, a Hydro Quebec bill, a lot of drums (African and Irish), *hoisin* sauce, cans of house paint, books—Virgil, *The Cat in the Hat*, Spanish verbs, a guide to movies, a book in Russian—and a washboard. At least these are the things that first catch my eye.

I look out the window, and people zip about out there in the cold, bundled up, way beyond fretting about hat-head or a sleek silhouette. Restaurants and bars are packed. Friends gather everywhere. The city feels alive, born of a sure knowledge that this place, these frigid streets, the *sauce de poisson* and Hydro Quebec, all add up to a kind of heaven. Even without the caribou.

When we want to know how best to live, I think it helps to know what heaven could look like. Maybe it has something to do with teaching four-year-olds in the local shelter what a platypus looks like; or seeing great Chinese vases; or getting back in touch with the old neighbors, or spiritual practice, or the folks at AA. Kicking up your heels at a very loud party or a big family dinner, a solo hike to a place with a view, or baking those delicious, to-die-for éclairs again. When thinking about how to live life, a picture of heaven can be a part of the recipe.

Among the gazillions of other spiritual strategies, I would mention one more:

When the plan changes, relax.

I love the author Calvin Trillin, and in his book *Family Man* he describes a scene where he is seated next to a friend's eleven-year-old, Molly, at brunch at a café, when somebody says that the chef has "a great touch with omelets":

> Molly made the sort of face I became familiar with when our own children were around her age and someone at the dinner table carried on about some blissful experience with a wild mushroom or a raw oyster.
>
> Why did Molly grimace at the thought of eating eggs? Because several years before, she'd seen the most famous and widely praised drug com-

mercial in the anti-drug campaign. The commercial opens with a shot of a raw egg, while a voice says, "'This is your brain." The egg is then dumped onto a sizzling griddle while the voice says, "This is your brain on drugs." The commercial may well have put a number of teen-agers off drugs. It put at least one six-year-old in New Jersey off eggs.

Trillin calls this "the doctrine of unintended consequences."

It may be an odd idea, but I believe that fully human, spiritual people understand and accept this doctrine. There is a serenity that comes from realizing that the best laid plans can just as easily result in an eleven-year-old who won't eat eggs. It seems to me that healthy people find a way of accepting the "good try," the "best shot."

You insisted on music lessons for your child—you pictured her accompanying the church choir—but your child turns around and becomes an orange-haired body-pierced aspiring rock star in Las Vegas. All because of those music lessons—that's not what you meant to do! You pictured yourself living in L.A. by now, what with your college major in film, but your niche turned out to be cable TV sales, and you live in Minneapolis, where it snows. That wasn't exactly the intention. You went for couples counseling to strengthen your relationship, only to conclude that really, the two of you have always been poorly suited. The doctrine of unintended consequences.

Looking around, I notice that people who feel content about their lives are people who relax in the face of the changed plan, who keep a sense of humor about life's absurdities—even the cruel tricks—and get on with life.

Living life. Whether it's dealing gracefully with the unintended consequence, moving a little closer to heaven, or using other guidelines and metaphors entirely, as Unitarian Universalists we're free to choose a life. Not just free, I might add, but obliged. There's no doubt about it: In the midst of tying shoe laces, flipping pancakes, starting cars, and putting on our jackets, we create our lives. We can do it intentionally and well.

Out there in New Mexico, George and Evelyn Frey knew what it took: a piano and a pickup truck and a whole lot of trips along a very steep trail. Maybe it seemed crazy. But it was life as they wanted to live it, it connected them to what they knew to be fundamental, and they made a lot of people happy along the way. May we choose as well.

Waiting It Out

Sometimes we—any of us—get into some kind of mess, large or small, where there really is nothing we can do. Not a thing. We are not fully in command. We have to find the courage to just wait it out.

Edna O'Brien once wrote an essay called "Waiting":

> We wait for money; we wait for the weather to get warmer, colder; we wait for the plumber to come and fix the washing machine; we wait for a friend to give us the name of another plumber; we wait for our hair to grow; we wait for our children outside school; we wait for their exam results; we wait for the letter that will undo all desolation; we wait for Sunday, when we sleep in or have the extra piece of toast; we wait for the crocuses to come up, then the daffodils. . . . We wait for dreams, then we wait to be hauled out of our dreams and wait for dawn, the mail, tea, coffee, the first ring of the telephone, the advancing day.

We've all observed a whole catalog of ways of waiting in ourselves and in other people: There's the horticultural way of waiting, where you plant your perennial seeds in a little tray that balances on your window sill, and with a mild sense of anticipation, you wait for the slow ascent of the sprouts. There's the treading water way of waiting, where in some low-key way you work at it, steadily pumping your legs and moving your arms, swimming in place, checking off the minutes one by one until the test is over. Then there's the pacing the floor way of waiting—the frantic approach—where you pace around the room, or tap the table, or make those knitting needles fly, or bake three dozen cookies and make a pretty good dent in them, eating them as they cool. Of course, there's the worrying way of waiting: "Maybe she went to her friend Julie's house. And maybe on the way to Julie's—you know that awful steep hill? Maybe she fell off her bike. Or she was on her way to Julie's house and remembered she needed her social sciences book from school but the school was locked and she tried to break in and the police caught her and she's in jail." There's the "please-please-please" way of waiting—"Please-please-please let that college acceptance letter come today." There's the dreading way of waiting, too. "Ten days till the root canal. I'll bet it'll really hurt. Nine days till the root canal. I'll bet it'll really hurt. Eight days. . . ." You've seen the fantasy way of waiting: "Oh good, only an hour and a half till they announce the lottery winners. I wonder how late the travel agent stays open."

And finally, among the dozens and dozens of ways of waiting that any of us can think of, there's the angler's way of waiting. You get yourself out in a rowboat in a still pond, you bait your hook, and you sit there and wait. You don't feel one way or the other, particularly, about catching or not catching any fish. You sit there. You just sit there. Of all the ways of waiting, it seems to me this way, this image of the angler sitting in the rowboat holds the most promise of a calming—spiritual, if you will—way of waiting.

Some of us have a long-standing theological predisposition to believe in free will, so we are inclined to try to act in the face of adversity, to try to *do* something. Pelagius, in the fifth century, did us the favor of breaking away from the fatalistic, deterministic theology that suggests acceptance and waiting it out as the appropriate response to trouble. More often than not we preach a theology of empowerment, not waiting.

Maybe that's why waiting isn't my strong suit. Personally, I have tried out this whole list of ways of waiting. Sometimes all in one day. By happenstance, just once, on our family's sabbatical in Nepal some years ago, I got it right.

We had been hiking toward Mt. Everest for about eight days, so we were eight days from a road—not a road, really, but an airstrip of the sort you have to shoo the yaks off of before a little plane can land. Everything was great, except that our then-sixth-grader and I were sick.

We pitched the little back-packing tent, and Toby and I lay there to wait until we got better. The tent flaps were open to the Himalayan Mountain called Ama Dablam, and we waited there, watching the mountain and the clouds and sky that surrounded it. And we waited. Nothing hurt. We couldn't do anything. We didn't want anything. We couldn't eat anything. We just waited, there with the mountain. We just waited.

Toby and I both remember that period of waiting fondly. We felt completely at peace, surrounded by beauty. A peace, to be sure, created not by us but by a bug and a peculiar circumstance, but still, a useful lesson in waiting.

We got well, of course, after finally abandoning our American medicine and swallowing the who-knows-what-it-was medicine that the local people swear by. But sometimes while waiting in Boston traffic or late at night on tech-support hold, if not something more serious, I think of waiting in that tent, watching Ama Dablam, and I try to regain that mountain way of waiting.

You know the images that work for you when the waiting needs to settle in, whether they be as grand as a mountain or as simple as a cat in a sunny chair. May these images, these moments of waiting, be icons of peace and patience.

Carry-Ons for Life

I am traveling with eight feet of neoprene tubing, a blue plastic funnel, duct tape, a small trumpet mouthpiece, and, as logically follows, my husband, Chuck. Everyone has a list of travel essentials; if you're a horn player and you want to stay in shape, you can't leave home without your hosaphone.

The men of the Great Northern Exploration Expedition of 1860, the first outsiders to peek into Australia's interior, took a Chinese gong along, as well as a stationery cabinet, a heavy wooden table with matching stools, and fifteen hundred pounds of sugar. And even that is nothing compared to the packing list of one of the maharajahs from Jaipur, India, who, when traveling to England, filled two of the largest silver vessels on earth with water, and loaded them aboard. Why would he pack two containers of water the size of tool sheds? He didn't trust the quality of English water, so he brought his water from India, just to be safe.

Traveling separates us from most of our stuff. Freed of our laundry baskets and mysterious sets of extra keys—without the hammer, the dictionary, the floor lamp, the turkey baster; without so much as a tub to take a bath in—we have every reason to feel unencumbered, fleet of foot, and ready to go.

But no. Faced with the possibility of freedom, most humans find themselves wrangling the night before liftoff with urgent needs for the hosaphone, a Chinese gong, and our own vats of drinking water. We become hyper-materialists.

It's hard to let go—that's all I'm saying. We want to bring ourselves along on the trip, and how would we recognize ourselves without our stuff? Certainly that's the question travelers face, and it's not a bad question for life.

It comes up in various ways, this question of "stuff." Remember scenarios like this?

- ~ If you found yourself on a desert island with only three things, what would you want them to be?

- ~ If you won a contest where you could run around in a department store for a half hour choosing whatever you wanted, where would you head?

- ~ If you had two minutes to gather what would fit in a small carry-on before fleeing your house, what would you pack?

Rev. Peter Morales, UUA president, writes in his sermon "One Small Carry-On,"

> You have two minutes. You get to take the equivalent of one small carry-on. What few things do you grab as you run for your life?

When our lives are in danger and we risk losing everything, we cling first to those we love. Then we seize those things, like old family photos, that remind us of who we are and where we came from—things that connect us to special people.

In the Hebrew scriptures, a defining moment for the children of Israel came immediately after the Passover. Pharaoh tells the Hebrew people they can leave Egypt. In the story, the Israelites don't even wait for the bread to rise; they . . . leave at once. This is their chance at freedom, their opportunity to create a new future. They don't hesitate.

They grab what they can and head out. . . .

In order to move on in our lives, in order to seize the promise that the future holds, we have to learn to leave unnecessary baggage behind. And unless you and I are willing to let go, to leave unessential things behind, we become prisoners of our past, shackled to our comforts, slaves to our possessions, in bondage to our habits. You and I can never reach our promised land, we never attain the promise that lies within us, unless we are willing to leave behind the fleshpots of bondage and risk the unknown.

You and I get one small carry-on. We can only take what we can carry with us. What shall we take into our future? What shall we leave behind?

Whether we consider the question literally or metaphorically, clarity about our identity, our values, and our spiritual good health allows us to move toward freedom. Is it time to abandon the family farm in order to break free and study ballet? Can we leave our identity as a victim behind, having healed enough to feel whole and strong for the future? Does freedom for you mean committing to the job you love, finally leaving the volunteer work? Or committing to the volunteer work, finally leaving the job? Maybe we start small: We're simply getting the extraneous stuff out of the basement, out of the email folders, or out of the trunk of the car, keeping only the one or two treasures.

For those in the Passover story, the focus was freedom. They could only take what nourished them as they rushed to their future. The freedom we move toward is a different, more luxurious freedom, and, much of the time, we can take what we want to take. May we choose what nourishes us.

Stepping Off the Platform and Other Sabbatical Escapades

From time to time, ministers take sabbatical time to regroup. For me, some kind of jolting adventure does the trick, and I always return to ministry with new eyes.

I spent my most recent sabbatical in Panama, hoping that in spite of advancing post-polio symptoms, I could still engage in an escapade or two. Well. There's nothing like dugout canoes, zip lines, snorkels, and rafts to fill that bill. And Central American hammocks afforded a great opportunity to give the muscles a break. In the spirit of gratitude, I offer you five sabbatical pieces.

I Got a Boat

He says it in English: "I got a boat." Those are the last words we understand. So we know the young man has a boat and would like us to hire him to take us on a Sunday outing.

The boat is a standard local open boat with a small outboard motor, one sorry life-jacket, and one home-made paddle. We pay him three dollars and get in. He tells us to wait ten minutes—at least that's what we figure he told us. After a while, two more people join us and we set off.

We go, we tie up somewhere, someone holds the line while we wait for a long time in choppy seas. Then a family climbs in—with four little children. They hand me the baby while they get themselves organized. It begins to rain.

Again we go, this time for a long time, and occasionally this question forms in our minds: "Where to?" And then we arrive at a jungle beach—clear skies now—mangroves and palms and dense and vigorous green stuff in all shapes and sizes, a place complete with a real McCoy jungle sound track.

We go over the side into the shallow salt lagoon, floating in clear water among dozens of orange starfish the size of Frisbees. A dolphin and her baby describe perfect arcs nearby.

Seven hours later we, this boatload of strangers, kiss each other goodbye.

If I Saw Me Coming Up the River

It really doesn't matter where you are, and aging makes it worse: If you look anything like me, the farther you paddle up-river in a dugout canoe, the more conspicuous you become. You are a tourist. Sure, you could be a life-long missionary or a career-change Peace Corps volunteer, but getting pegged as a tourist is a pretty safe bet.

If I lived in this village I would essentially wear nothing at all—maybe a cloth folded around my midsection, and a few beads. I would feel nice and cool, and somehow the jungle insects and the power of the sun wouldn't bother me.

Instead I am wearing light-weight pants bathed in some kind of toxic bug-repellant-solar-blocking agent. I wear shoes. And all the rest: a little hat, a Cool-Max shirt, a day pack. My skin is light and my eyes are blue. In this environment, I look ridiculous even to myself.

If I saw me coming up the river, I would see an intrusive source of money, pens, gum, and who knows what else. I would expect to get my picture taken whether I like it or not. I wouldn't want to see me coming.

I do arrive though, and some men approach who seem menacing to me. One of them begins to speak, and I don't know what to expect. I'm a little worried.

"Happy New Year, Tourist," is what he says with a warm smile, and the men continue on their way.

Stepping Off the Platform

You step into a zip line harness, put the thick gloves on, snap a series of clips onto a cable, and you're ready to step off the platform. Seems like the best way to get a good look at the jungle life, the dramatic waterfall, and whatever goes on in the tree canopy, without tromping through the forest with a machete.

There is nothing about this setup, however, that inspires confidence. Certainly no inspection certificate framed on the wall of the small open-air shack where the equipment is stored. And I wouldn't have had the language skills to absorb Panamanian safety instructions, had there been any. Plus, the zip lines, a series of four, are really high up!

But there is no going back, so I get my eyeballs prepared, my camera ready, and my spirit open, eager to get to the part where the jungle comes alive to me in a series of transformational moments.

I step off the platform, and begin to zip down the first line, lickety-split. At the outset, one significant observation does break through to me as though writ large, but it isn't the kind of spiritual observation I was really looking for: "Grip the cable behind you with all your might, or you will spin out of control."

OK, never mind. I have another chance at a momentous awakening in these extraordinary natural surroundings.

Zip line #2. Step off the platform. Whoosh. Another bolt from above, and the words form in my head, "If you don't grip those cables harder, you will hit the tree at the end at a zillion miles an hour. Do not flub this up."

Zip line #3. Step off the platform. Way up, zooming now over the waterfall. I'm pretty sure it is lovely in a blurred sort of way.

Zip line #4. Step off the platform. The thought of looking for monkeys or tapirs or capybaras or toucans never enters my mind. I will never feel one with the jungle by way of zip lines, of this I am now sure. And clearly, I am not transformed.

Unless you count flying over the jungle, free of everything you know. Unless you count feeling small amidst a universe of unseen teaming life. Unless you count wanting to live to see another day.

It Lasts a Long Time

Into the dim hut I go. They are all there, the grandmother, an aunt, a young mother—way young—and a newborn little girl. Dirt floor, hammocks.

They check me out—my pierced earrings to their nose rings, my jeans to their red and orange beaded leg bands, my blue T-shirt to the intricate molas on their blouses, my tan baseball cap to their yellow headscarves, my plain nose, a little sunburned, to the delicate black patterns on theirs.

I was clearly found lacking in the glamour department.

So they set to decorating my nose.

Using a jagua fruit and a tiny stick, grandma made quick work of it.

Everybody happy.

You would think, wouldn't you, that this stuff would wash off, that in fairly short order persistent nose-scrubbing would ease me back into a civilization I recognize.

You would think, wouldn't you, that jagua geometrics go only skin deep.

You would think, wouldn't you, that a visit to a hut would wear off quickly.

But it lasts a long time.

The Panama Hat

The Panama hats in the village outdoor market are tempting, but too touristy, don't you think? Chuck kind of wanted one, but instead we signed up for a raft trip.

Didn't think much about it. This raft trip would be longer than most and wilder—along the Rio Chirique Viejo on the Costa Rican/Panamanian border—"nonstop excitement" didn't scare us—we'd rafted before.

Such a sunny day to paddle through the jungle scenery, and exhilarating rapids, even the Class IV's seemed manageable. But after an hour or two the worst happened, the raft flipped, and we were in the water smack in the middle of the most dangerous rapids on the river.

I knew immediately that I might not survive, that I should keep my wits, and I should draw in my arms and legs so they wouldn't break against the rocks. I needed to let the helmet and life jacket do whatever there was to do. I had been told that in a flip situation I would not know which way was up during the process of being tossed around so forcefully, that I would not be able to breathe for a very long time, and I would take in a lot of water. All true.

Of course it seemed to take forever, but I did land in calmer water, and I began to hear, ever so faintly, a voice calling "Señora! Señora!" And then I am rescued. I try to get my lungs organized for breathing, and scan for my partner of more than forty years, Chuck. Soon he is rescued too, and at last each of us knows the other is alive.

We are still near the beginning of the raft trip, and inexplicably, we paddle for hours down the rest of the river in high spirits. Through a dramatic cold, pelting rainstorm—and rapids and more rapids—somehow a "can-do" spirit emerged, and by the end of the day, feeling good, we were wondering what we could find for snacks.

If you had seen me twenty-four hours later in the Panama City airport headed for home right on schedule, you would have seen a sobered woman, limping and black-and-blue, her hair standing on end, glad to be alive. At one of the airport shops, she was buying a Panama hat.

The next day, back at work, people asked about my trip. "Good trip," I said. "Bought a Panama hat. Life is short."

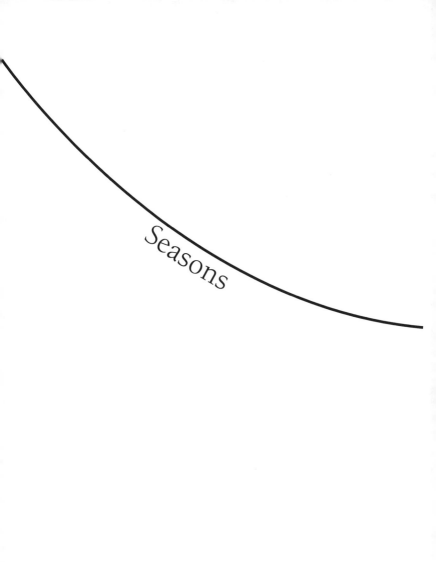

Seasons

The Clear, Dark, Lovely Whistler and Other Small Epiphanies

There's nothing better than an epiphany. If I had to choose a favorite among traditional Christian theological terms—*atonement, confession, sacrament, grace, incarnation, repentance*—that kind of list, I'd pick epiphany. Yet come January, when Epiphany shows up on the liturgical calendar, I hesitate to mention it. Who wants to hear about three kings, a star, and a stable once the holiday season is over?

The word, of course, has changed in meaning over the years. No longer limited to "a celebration of the divine nature of Jesus as represented by the Magi," these days anybody can have an epiphany over just about anything. Technically, divinity is not a requirement. Yet the foundational story still grabs me.

The Christian scriptures offer a good start. Though the wise men aren't kings at the biblical stage, people later filled in the details, giving the wise men (three now in number) regal status, home countries, and physical descriptions. The three kings find the little baby, and they fall on their knees in wonder and awe. The first epiphany.

While religious purists surely lament that the word *epiphany* has wandered away from the crèche, I appreciate the chance to enjoy epiphanies on a more regular basis. Sometimes they're little. Really, very little. Like discovering that the yellow finches show up if the thistle seed is fresh and the feeder's in an auspicious spot. The spring turns the males as yellow as crayons. This epiphany is hardly on the scale of a divine newborn baby—yet it's not altogether different. In my book, the sudden awareness of yellow finches qualifies as an epiphany. To meet the criterion, the experience has to point to the wonder of it all.

Sure, I've had my small share of sudden insights— flashes of lucidity whereby I unexpectedly overcome the software glitch, or it dawns on me in the nick of time that this person and that person are more than just friends, or I finally figure out how to extract the key from the ignition of a rental car. But those are merely moments where the brain kicks in; they are not apprehensions of anything like the divine, however defined—they are not epiphanies.

The poet Mary Oliver once wrote about her partner,

All of a sudden she began to whistle. By all of a sudden I mean that for more than thirty years she had not whistled. It was thrilling. At first I wondered, who was in the house, what stranger? I was upstairs reading, and she was downstairs. As from the throat of a wild and cheerful bird, not caught but visiting, the sounds warbled and slid and doubled back and larked and soared.

Finally I said, Is that you? Is that you whistling? Yes, she said. I used to whistle, a long time ago.

Now I see I can still whistle. And cadence after cadence she strolled through the house, whistling.

I know her so well, I think. I thought. Elbow and ankle. Mood and desire. Anguish and frolic. Anger too. And the devotions. And for all that, do we even begin to know each other? Who is this I've been living with for thirty years?

This clear, dark, lovely whistler?

To be stunned into poetry by the whistling of a loved one is the kind of epiphany I'm looking for. That kind of jolt. Predicated on receptivity, openness, welcome.

I wish I could sign up for twelve months of epiphanies, along the lines of the fruit-of-the-month club. Perhaps for January, the sudden sure knowledge that snowfall is unutterably striking. The newspaper story in February that knocks me over with the kindness implied. The smell of the mud that hits in March, catapulting me into an awareness of the earth below my feet. And so it would go without money-back guarantees, but a worthy program nonetheless.

They don't have to be about kings, these epiphanies of ours, or Jesus. It's enough that they glue us to something dear—the whistler, the yellow finch.

The Tough Times and the Glorious

Sooner or later, because we are human, our souls and spirits ache. Sometimes the aching settles down into a yearning. Sometimes, way down beneath our living out the day, we feel only traces of a gentle longing, but still, somewhere inside, over time, we feel the ache of people everywhere.

Religion is supposed to help with that. Sure, it's easy enough for religion to jump in with celebrations, but can it recognize the tougher times? I want to mention three of these universal longings.

First, it seems to me, there is a part of each of us that wants to be cared for, to know we'll be provided for. I'm talking about security at its most basic. We would appreciate knowing for sure, for example, that we will never go hungry, even if we become very old, or very sick, or very unlucky. And if we move beyond the aching to know that *we* will be OK, we uncover concern for the people we love, and the people of the past and present and on into the future who don't have and will never have a fraction of what they need.

Secondly, none of us is happy with ourselves all of the time. And other people aren't always happy with us. That's just how it is. For everybody. How nice it would be for some cosmic presence—or even just a person whom you trust—to assure you each night as you drifted off to sleep that even though you may have turned your back on someone you care about, even though you may have raised children who disappointed you, even though you may have betrayed someone badly, even though there's not a chance you can deliver what you promised—in spite of all that, you are forgiven and loved. And equally, wouldn't it be wonderful if, when someone has neglected you or let you down, hurt you, or disappointed you, you could find a way to move on? A second common yearning is to be able to forgive and be forgiven.

A third kind of ache is the fear of crumbling in the face of life's trials. We don't have any idea what's ahead. We see outlandish tragedy and moral ambiguity all around us. If disaster (or further disaster) or temptation should come our way, could we stand up to it? Would we have what it takes to move through the crisis with strength of character, courage, and grace?

The fact is, we aren't ever really secure in life. Neither we nor the people around us will live up to all of our expectations, and life may require us to cope with more than we feel able to bear. Sadly, that's just the way it is. And it's old, old, news.

The prayer known as the Lord's Prayer, or Jesus' Prayer, contains three active requests: for bread, forgiveness, and strength—the three timeless longings I mentioned above. "Give us this day our daily bread, And forgive us our trespasses as we forgive those who trespass against us, And lead us not into temptation, but deliver us from evil." It turns out that over the ages, we humans are in the business of being human together, and lo and behold, the sentiments expressed in that section of the Lord's Prayer are shared on some level by most of us today.

To be sure, Unitarian Universalists have a wide variety of responses to Jesus' Prayer in its entirety. For some, it's a central spiritual resource. Others disagree with many of the actual words, but love the sound of it. Some object to the exclusively masculine imagery found in the familiar translations, while others have miserable childhood associations with the recitation of the words. Still others find that the prayer means nothing to them. I did not grow up knowing this prayer, and while I can't imagine myself fully embracing a prayer that begins with anthropomorphic imagery and a passive approach to life, I do appreciate the connection I feel with an ancient people who felt a need for bread, and forgiveness, and strength.

As far as we know, Jesus believed in praying spontaneously from the heart. He would not have recognized the liturgical evolution and translation that resulted in "Our Father who art in heaven," or "Thine is the kingdom and the power and the glory forever and ever." But he probably would have recognized the universal needs behind the body of the prayer.

When Christians recognize Good Friday and Easter in the space of three days they acknowledge the worst of times and the best. Here we have a religion that really does embrace the range of human experience. And isn't that religion's job?

Unitarian Universalists have a lot of latitude when it comes to religious expression, and Easter time is no exception. Acknowledging the tough times and the glorious, whether through images of autumn death and new life in spring, the dark days before the summer sun, or the death and return to life of Jesus is an assignment for all of us.

Our Kind of Story

Most Unitarian Universalists were not raised in Unitarian Universalism. Some were, but the rest of you came to this religious home from someplace else. As the spring holidays approach, I imagine your backgrounds and experiences, and how you might relate to Easter. Some of you come from the Jewish tradition, and Easter seems either beside the point or a downright imposition. Others of you have entirely secular backgrounds, or you were raised outside the Western tradition, and you may or may not have particular feelings one way or the other. The vast majority of today's Unitarian Universalists were raised Protestant or Catholic or Orthodox—and for you Easter carries a charge that plays itself out in a vast array of positive, negative, or mixed emotions.

Others of you spent these holidays in Unitarian or Universalist or UU sanctuaries, experiencing a Christian perspective, perhaps, or Humanist, or a broad-based inclusivity, and for you the holidays range from "no big deal" to one of the year's major highlights.

Almost all of you have a prior relationship with a man called Jesus. Some of you pray to him or relate to him as your friend. Some of you grew tired of hearing about him as children or live in a geographical area of constant Jesus-chatter, and you don't want to hear another word about him. Some of you are angry at Jesus, or angry at the churches you associate with him. For some of you Jesus is God. He may be your teacher or your role model. For most of you, Jesus is a part of your childhood and he is alive in your memories. He may arise from the depths of your psyche in the middle of a long dark night, or he may figure in your decision-making day-to-day. For many of you, Jesus is a central figure at Easter time, present for you by virtue of your upbringing, in the customs, smells, burdens, and delights of the Easter season.

What does your current relationship with Jesus look like? What comes to mind when Jesus is mentioned? Where to begin?

Jesus was a Galilean Jew. Most men had beards at the time; Jesus probably did too. Many men wore their hair long in a braid down their backs—maybe that's what Jesus did. We would expect him to have had dark hair, dark eyes. He would have eaten with his hands from a common bowl, as dishes were expensive. He no doubt wore his clothes many days in a row. He would not have brushed his teeth. Ordinarily, the men of his time did not talk with women in public, and men danced with men, and women with women. Their life expectancy was thirty-seven years.

We have no reason to believe that Jesus thought himself to be the Messiah, the Savior, the Lord, or in any way divine—these were ideas later ascribed to him by his followers. He is silent as well, scholars say, on the subjects of heaven and hell, resurrection, the end of the world, the last judgment, and angels.

Most Unitarian Universalists find it easy to imagine this kind of human Jesus. But at this time of year, we don't get off quite so easily, because the resurrection shows up on our calendars on Easter Day. What are we to do?

You may find it interesting to take a look at the Gospel According to Mark, the earliest of the four Gospels in the Christian scriptures, written about seventy years after Jesus' birth. It's a compilation of the oral tradition that already existed about Jesus.

In Mark, Jesus is crucified, and after the Sabbath, Mary Magdalene and Mary set off to find his body to anoint it: "As they entered the tomb, they saw a young man, dressed in a white robe, sitting on the right side; and they were alarmed. But he said to them, 'Do not be alarmed; you are looking for Jesus of Nazareth, who was crucified. He has been raised; he is not here.'"

Scholars agree that the true Gospel According to Mark ends with the women fleeing in terror (Mark 16:8). The two Marys don't tell a soul, and Jesus never shows up again. Wow!

Imagine if the early Christians had let that story stay in print as it was first told, ending as it did in a frightened failure of nerve.

It took a couple hundred years, but finally someone did add another twelve verses to Mark. Now, at the end of the story, Jesus appears again as if he were not dead.

Some people think that resurrection has to be about the resuscitation of a corpse. Of course not. Dead people don't come back to life. At least that's not our kind of story.

For us, it's like this: We know that when something as wonderful as the message of Jesus comes along, in real life it does not die forever. The message comes back to life. We know that when goodness, and righteousness, and love emerge in the midst of humanity, they continue to rise up and come back to us. We know that hope does not die; hope comes back to life. And so it was with Jesus in the story. It was as if he were not dead. That's the kind of story that can grab us and hold us. In our kind of story, that is resurrection.

No Bad Dancers

Sometimes, in the closets of churches—way in the back—you'll find long, gauzy scarves in a variety of colors. They've been there a long time, and I remember why. From time to time, liturgical dance becomes popular in congregations, and one such period was the 1950s. We wanted our young people to express themselves, we wanted to nurture their creativity, we wanted them to enjoy their bodies, we wanted them to experience firsthand the variety of forms that religion could take.

So it was that I spent seven years bounding about barefooted in rented elementary school gyms on Wednesday afternoons. Dancing "the Good Samaritan" was my specialty, and while the Unitarians certainly had "no bad dancers" among their youth, I wasn't very good. But I was a springy sort of a child, so I could leap, and I enjoyed employing this unusual gait in the service of traveling from Jerusalem to Jericho.

Our teacher seemed simultaneously frail and sturdy. She had orange hair, and she arrived from the city every week with her cheerful round partner and a long-suffering piano player who knew just what to do even though he couldn't see. While I absorbed a lot about Unitarian values, embodiment, and religion, I feel quite sure that our performances did nothing for those who watched.

In fact, truth be told, I myself had never experienced a lick of inspiration by watching liturgical dance until recently, when I visited a downtown African American mega-church in Dallas, Texas.

During the service, when nobody expected it, about a dozen 14-year-old boys of all shapes and sizes, wearing what they wear these days, emerged from various pews among the congregation, moving in a liturgical dance to the rhythms provided by the gospel choir. They seemed unaware of those of us who watched; they were authentic in their physical testimony, and unabashed. It was as if the Junior Varsity football team suddenly took to dancing its religion in church, glad to do it.

One of the functions of religion is to offer renewal, hope, and a certain lightness of heart, particularly at this time of year. We are looking for a sense of freedom, an optimism about what comes next. During the course of the boys' dance, I felt it all: Easter, Passover, and the new life of spring, rolled into one.

I never know when it will happen, this spring holiday feeling, or why. Maybe for you it shows up when you observe a special kindness from a cashier, or when the crab apple tree blooms—the one you planted when your brother died—or when the piece you've been practicing on the piano turns out just perfect, or when the baby sleeps through the night. Maybe you're in church, and the sermon and music work together just right, or you change medication and experience an unexpected new lease on life. A clever bit on the Comedy Channel, favorite poetry on your bookshelf, new love, or a clean house, finally. For me, this time, it was a moment of liturgical dance.

This isn't to say that life's finally going to be great—I know that our time on earth is not all flowering crab apple trees and gestures of kindness from cashiers. There's no denying the rough spots, and, as we've all heard too often, it's the contrast between difficult times and joy that allows us our Easters, Passovers, and equinox celebrations. Wislawa Szymborska puts it plainly in her poem, "Theater Impressions," which highlights the curtain call:

> For me the tragedy's most important act is the sixth:
> The raising of the dead from the stage's battlegrounds,
> The straightening of wigs and fancy gowns,
> removing knives from stricken breasts,
> taking nooses from lifeless necks,
> lining up among the living
> to face the audience.

During the spring holidays, at least in the northern hemisphere, ideally, that's what happens. The nooses and knives go away, we spiff up our gowns and wigs, and take our places across the stage, with happiness and hope, among the living.

As Unitarian Universalists, we enjoy full freedom to make the most of our holidays. Whatever you are celebrating at this time of year, may the dead parts turn to life within, in whatever way you prefer, to face the freedom and new awakening that lies ahead.

Hooray for stories. The knee-slapper story you hear at a party; the astonishing story that widens your world; the quiet snuggly bedtime story; the heartwarming story that gives you hope, inspiration, or motivation; even the story that raises an eyebrow. There are a gazillion kinds of stories, and most of them we like.

Does that include the Passover story and the Easter story? Sure it does. For years I've preached, along with my colleagues in the Unitarian Universalist ministry, that stories bear truths. And that's a fundamental part of what Unitarian Universalism's all about, the "free and responsible search for truth."

But then I went to the Science Museum here in Boston, and stumbled upon an exhibit about magic shows. Magic shows, of course, aren't at all about truth; they're about tricking people. And guess what the famous magicians Penn and Teller tell us is the essential basis for trickery? Stories! "The story is as important as the trick," they say. "The story helps you make sense of something you wouldn't ordinarily believe." And then the magician has you—you've been tricked into believing something just plain false.

OK. To state the obvious, just because it's a story—even a religious one, even one that's survived through the generations—certainly doesn't make the story true in any sense of the word. It doesn't necessarily point to metaphorical truth, nor does it necessarily convey ancient wisdom. The story might reflect an abiding truth, but it might as easily promote a destructive superstition or cruel ulterior motive. It might be a trick.

On the other hand, certainly a lot of stories, religious or not, are straight-up all to the good. And sometimes it just depends how the story is told. When I was a child, my school didn't have much of a grip on the separation between church and state, and so at this time of year we heard a lot about Jesus dying on the cross. I was a Unitarian, and this was the first I'd heard of the gory aspects of the crucifixion story—the nails in the palms and feet, the hours up there on the cross—the works. That he somehow rose straight up afterward didn't matter much to me. What I got out of the story told at school was a sick feeling in my stomach.

At church, the same story was not so much about nails and blood but about a good man's teachings living on after he was dead. His teachings came to life over and over again, not unlike the daffodil bulbs we planted in the autumn along the church's long driveway. Some might say this is simply a wimpier version of the story, but it worked for me.

There was another difference between what I learned in school and what I learned in Sunday school: In school, the Easter narrative was presented as history; in Sunday school, as story.

To some Unitarian Universalists, it matters whether the basis of a religious story is historical, factual. It matters to a great many people, for example, whether Jesus did or did not come back to life after he died. Not wanting to be duped is a healthy part of human nature, and if the central story of a religion can't be shown to be literally true, many, reasonably, are unwilling to base their lives on it.

But some Unitarian Universalists find merit enough in the Jesus story to find inspiration or, indeed, a spiritual foundation. For them, the objective, historical truth doesn't matter one way or the other; what matters is the wisdom found in the long-standing legend. When a story offers a basis for hope, health, celebration, and good works, why not call it a keeper?

You probably have your own sources of stories that serve you well, that you remember with gratitude and a smile, that lie beneath your life to help to make it stable. Maybe it's the story of a great man named Jesus who rose from the dead, or an ancient story where slaves move to freedom. Maybe it's family stories about Ellis Island, or a prayer shawl handed down, or pine saplings hauled out West in a trunk. Or the biography of a famous ball player or astronomer. Or some tale your barber told you once about a customer who showed courage, or promise, or spunk.

You are the person who decides which stories are your religious stories, which seem like trickery and which speak to you as higher truths. You—with your passions and your quirks and your particular preferences—are the person who chooses the stories for your life, the stories that buoy and sustain you, alert and amuse you, and fill your spirit.

Hooray for stories.

Language of the People

Spring holidays. Images of journeys. The Exodus out of Egypt as Passover nears, Jesus making his Palm Sunday approach, and our own journeys through life. It can feel like the *Canterbury Tales*, the "Prologue," where in the springtime you take to your feet and you make the journey, the journey that matters the most.

As soon as April pierces to the root
The drought of March, and bathes each bud and
    shoot
Through every vein of sap with gentle showers
From whose engendering liquor spring the
    flowers. . . .

Life stirs their hearts and tingles in them so,
Then people long on pilgrimage to go,
And palmers to set out for distant strands
And foreign shrines renowned in sundry lands.

There are times in life ripe for the journey. Sometimes, of course, there is little choice. Refugees run for their lives, carrying heavy toddlers, fleeing to who knows what kind of a life. When the time came for the ancient Hebrews to leave Egypt, they couldn't think twice and wait for the bread to rise, they just went. The journey was no spiritual metaphor for them, it was the harshest of concrete realities.

But for most of us the journey, the pilgrimage, can be a choice. We have that luxury. Like the pilgrims headed to Canterbury, we can take the summer camping trip to that special place where we feel our spirits restored. We can walk to our favorite personal sacred spot in the town forest; we can search out, many of us, the places where our grandmothers were born or where the sunsets are so spectacular or where the early bulbs come up, and feel a new sense of grounding.

Or maybe the journey is purely metaphorical: a spiritual journey of self-awareness or of healing after a difficult childhood or troublesome relationship. Perhaps the journey is an escape from a job that confined the spirit or it's leaving behind a life that did not reflect who you were at all. Maybe it involves a foray into a new field of expertise, new classes, new skills. You might create an intentional family of nurturing friends or you might find your way to a new sense of peace and service and satisfaction. First the escape, then the journey.

This escape from bondage to freedom is, of course, the story told in the story of Passover.

For four-hundred years the ancient Hebrews were enslaved in Egypt. Moses was told by God in the form of a burning bush to lead his people out of Egypt. Moses paid Pharaoh a little visit, commanding, "Let my people go." Pharaoh didn't take kindly to the idea.

So God sent plagues—frogs and locusts and all the rest—and finally, the horrific killing of the Egyptian first-born babies, while the Hebrew babies were passed over. At this point Pharaoh finally set the Israelites free, and they fled in haste, before he changed his mind.

But of course he did change his mind, and his troops chased the Israelites in chariots and on horses, and when the Israelites were tempted to give in, Moses parted the Red Sea, and the Israelites walked to freedom.

This year what has taken hold of me about Passover is not so much the story itself, but the very fact that the story is reliably told and retold, generation after generation, at the family Seder. The story is a fundamental part of the language of a people. It provides the basis for religious identity, and helps to preserve the community, sustaining an enduring culture and tradition.

The whole story is about freedom, but what I'm thinking about just now is how over the centuries the Jews maintain their journey toward freedom as a group with definite boundaries, a religious group, and they continue doing that in spite of enormous odds against them. We read of Jewish soldiers in the U.S. Civil War, who on Passover managed to hold a Seder, substituting bricks for the mixture of apples and nuts that are customary, and a wild weed for the bitter herb. In the Warsaw ghetto during World War II, Jews conducted Seders from memory. Even in the concentration camps Jewish prisoners were reluctant to eat leavened bread during Passover.

I don't know whether any of us has experienced this kind of deprivation or this kind of longing for the practices of our people. But we can probably understand the feeling of wanting a recognizable anchor when we're feeling adrift in our own small ways. A colleague of mine, Rev. Emily Gage, tells about being in the Peace Corps in Poland when she heard that a McDonald's was opening in Warsaw:

It wasn't as if we didn't like the food [in Poland]. Over the months I had come to adore *pierogi*, filled with cheese or mushrooms or blueberries. I ate cabbage and potatoes and strawberries prepared in ways I never dreamed possible. I even developed a great fondness for beets. And one particular day, after a long hiking expedition, we reached a hut at the bottom of a mountain. There I sat down and ate one of the best bowls of *bigos*—a stew full of sauerkraut and kielbasa—that I had ever eaten. I had hiked just long enough and it had cooked just long enough to make it the perfect match of a meal.

Still, my thoughts turned to the golden arches.

One day, miraculously, there they were.

I sat down amidst the crowds, and took a bite out of my cheeseburger. And, I kid you not, tears came to my eyes. Not because it was particularly delicious, no, but because this cheeseburger tasted exactly like every other McDonald's cheeseburger I had ever eaten. And here it was in the midst of this strange country, where everything had been new. This cheeseburger was a soothing blanket of familiarity that fed my soul, so long trying to sort out the chaos of living in a foreign country. I felt renewed in a way I had not thought possible—not by the food really, but by this nourishment of connection to my past, to my country, to the rest of the world.

Lest you think I'm comparing the Passover Seder to a McDonald's hamburger, let me point out that it is this feeling, this "nourishment of connection to the past," not the burger itself, that I am talking about here. The Seder is the language of the Jewish people. This aspect, this identity-preservation aspect of Passover caught my attention by a circuitous route.

A couple years back some of the communities northwest of Boston were blanketed by a mass mailing attacking Unitarian Universalists. Every resident of half a dozen suburbs received a respectable looking twelve-page document. The headline read: "Unitarians attack Jews and Christians," not realizing that in large part we *are* Jews and Christians, and we were in the midst of celebrating the Jewish and Christian holidays.

It claimed that "militant homosexual activists" took control of the Unitarian Universalist Association in 1970, and it's been downhill ever since. It said we show pornography to fifth graders. It said that in 1933 we banned God from our churches. It said we're on the slippery slope, heading toward the likes of Stalin and Hitler.

And you know what else? It proclaimed that with regard to our stand on homosexuality, we won't budge.

That we go on and on and on about how we believe in the inherent worth and dignity of every human being.

Well, he got that one right. I don't see us negotiating about the fact that as religious people, Unitarian Universalists welcome everybody, as Jesus himself did. This is the kind of fundamental religious stance that we Unitarian Universalists take with us wherever we go—this is part of the language of our people, part of our identity, part of what we want to see live through the generations.

I told you that the re-telling of the Seder story caught my attention by means of a circuitous route, and this was it: The mass mailing got me to thinking about what enduring theological values are ours to hand down. If we were creating a ritual meal like a Seder, what would it be about?

At first, of course, when you come into Unitarian Universalism, you notice the freedom. No pretending you believe in a doctrine that inside you have doubts about. No guilt about not believing or about not coming to church. No hierarchy. There really is a lot of freedom. While we recognize that, for most Americans, theological freedom may not be a high priority when it comes to religion, and we fully support those who feel comfortable in doctrinal religions, creeds and doctrines are just not our particular way.

Occasionally a ministerial intern will focus on the freedom that we have in Unitarian Universalism, so I quickly give that intern an annoying assignment: Write a reflection paper about our theological limits. The intern usually says there are no limits: "We're free." And then I ask, "Can you as a UU minister lead worship by sacrificing chickens? Is that recognizable as Unitarian Universalism? Can you conduct a service in Boston entirely in Hebrew or Arabic or Tibetan? Is that Unitarian Universalism? Can you do a Trinitarian baptism, absolving an infant of original sin? Is that Unitarian Universalism? Where is the line? What is 'the language of our people'? What pieces of theological identity are we promoting and protecting? If we were forced to leave our homes as a group and head for the promised land, what common practices would we take along?"

I could make a very long list, but I'll name just six examples, all born of one historical and denominational period. When Unitarians set out on their theological journey toward independence in the early 1800s in New England, they broke away from the established religion of the day. What they stood for during their break for independence, and what we still stand for (among other things from other parts of our history), are these:

- ∾ If we believe in a god at all, we believe in a benevolent god, not a frightening or punishing god. That's something Unitarian Universalists carry with us on our journeys.

- ∾ We believe in the humanity of Jesus, whom we view as a wise and wonderful teacher, but not a god. That's something Unitarian Universalists carry with us.

~ We reject the doctrine of innate depravity. We do not believe in original sin—that becomes crystal clear when you listen to the words of our child dedications. We carry the theology of potential goodness with us.

~ We believe in free will, not predestination. Events are not preordained nor "meant to be." We have the power to act in the world. We carry that free will with us as Unitarian Universalists.

~ We believe in the freedom of conscience, that creeds do not serve us well. We carry that freedom of conscience with us on our journey.

~ And we believe in the use of reason as part of determining personal religious truth. We carry that use of reason with us always.

We carry other aspects of identity with us too: the flaming chalice, our hymns, our rejection of the Trinity, our personal approach to memorial services and funerals, our self-governance, our commitment to social justice in the world here and now, our reverence for nature, our love of community. They are not Passover matzohs, or palm fronds. They are not written in Middle English, they are not MacDonald's hamburgers, but they are ours. When we go on our journeys, they are ours to take along.

May we carry them with us, that they may offer us solace when we need it, inspiration when the world seems dull, challenge when we are lulled into complacency, and the seeds of love and friendship when we feel alone in the world.

The Beastly Practices of the Mad Bacchanalians

What a scandal it was! The season was spring, the year, 1627. The outrage involved eighty vertical feet of pine, so the story goes. The Pilgrims had erected a Maypole.

As Nathaniel Hawthorne imagined it in his story "The May-Pole of Merry Mount," a silken banner streamed from the top, colored like a rainbow, and a wild throng gathered 'round with minstrels, wandering players, mummers, and rope-dancers. A real convention of mirth-makers. And they danced!

Well. The Puritans in the neighborhood—their tastes running more toward stocks and whipping-posts—did not approve. They assaulted the Maypole with their "keen swords," and in short order, down it fell.

There we have it. Myles Standish, the well-known nondancer, nonsinger, and noncelebrator, gathered America's first vice squad and called a quick halt to what were later termed "the beastly practices of the mad Bacchanalians."

Hundreds of years later, the incident comes across to many as a battle between the fun-lovers and the prudes, though historically, complexities came into play involving theology, indentured servants, wilderness justice, free elections, guns, food distribution, and the beaver trade. For some, however, here in the twenty-first century, the interesting aspect of the Maypole discussion is ritual.

I recently had the humbling experience of stumbling upon a sermon I wrote in 1980 on the topic of ritual. In the seventies, ritual had been a hot topic in Unitarian Universalist circles, and I figured I'd wrap the topic up.

I carefully established that at their best, rituals celebrate and define life at every level—they surround birth, love, work, politics, social change. We construct rituals in and around sickness, sorrow, separation, and death. We anchor our realities. Of course, I quickly distanced myself from the sanctimonious, and any hint of hocus-pocus. Me? I was all for ritual that points toward the great realities of life—symbolic actions that have dimensions of depth within the human soul, religious or not. I granted that the ritual might be happy or solemn, secular or sacred, personal or institutional, public or private, but whatever the case, it needed to be deeply touching, a signal of transcendence. I would soon turn thirty.

"Deeply touching, a signal of transcendence"? Apparently in my younger days my attitude toward ritual was pretty highfalutin. I have to admit that I came down a little hard at that time on rituals that didn't appeal to me personally—secret handshakes, the Miss America Pageant, Thanksgiving Day football games, paper hats, noisemakers, and, okay, forced frivolity around a May-pole, to name a few. But by now I have been around a few blocks and have watched people here and there in the world ground themselves through rituals of pouring water, offering fruit to statues, spinning around, blowing horns, floating little boats, arranging stones in great piles, and yes, putting on special hats. Chanting, dancing, sitting, kneeling, washing, burning, dunking, piercing, hallucinating, parading, fasting, prostrating, eating, circling—the list is long and the results often powerful. Determining whether a ritual is empty or sacred seems best left to the practitioner. I am much more open now.

On the other hand, some rituals seem either vaguely or explicitly destructive, and while Unitarian Universalists want to respect individuals and cultures that differ from each of our own, we don't want to make the case that anything goes.

How do we feel about the ritual exchange of mountains of expensive presents on Christmas morning? The crowning of a six-year-old at a beauty pageant? Communion—the body and blood? Ritual circumcision? Animal sacrifice? Maypoles? We each have a lot of choices to make.

Your spiritual inclinations may lead you to listening to church bells Sunday mornings if you have some nearby, Yoga, regular early morning walks, rocking the baby, calm reading time before sleep, lighting a chalice, a customary moment of gratitude, or conscious breathing during the morning commute. These days I'm not apt to list transcendence as an absolute requirement! Or you may be a perfectly deep, spiritual, kind and fun person whom ritual leaves cold. That's fine too. The freedom that Unitarian Universalists claim extends to ritual big-time. We're under no obligation; the choice is ours. We each have a cultural inheritance to acknowledge, a popular culture to react to, a family history to consider, and the great history and practice of Unitarians and Universalists to draw upon.

Begin, if you wish, with the Maypole.

Two Pockets

I never did graduate from high school. I didn't mean to not graduate, it's just that there was something in my high school about an Ohio history requirement, and I was an exchange student in Australia that year. It's been decades, and nobody has ever asked me if I've graduated from high school—it hasn't stopped me from further graduations—but I still half expect that someday soon some big guys will show up at my door and demand to see that high school diploma.

The fact that I myself did not graduate is the first of four reasons why I should not offer advice to you who are graduating or making transitions, even though it's part of my job as a minister.

The second reason why I should not give advice is that I don't know what you should do. I used to know what everybody should do, but after some years in the ministry, I have learned that I don't know what anybody should do unless they all but tell me.

People who care about you will tell you to major in math when you have the heart of a poet; they'll tell you to welcome children into your life early or late, when only you can know if and when you want to be a parent; people will try to tell you who to love and where you should work and how you should get the job in the first place. Then people will tell you whether to rent or save up for a house; they will give you advice about direct deposit, and house paint, and chimney sweeps and appliance repair, though what you may want is a motorbike and a sunny day, free of any address at all. And when you are old, people who are concerned about you will tell you not to drive anymore, to live in a smaller place, to get rid of a lot of your stuff, to give away your money. And though they love you all the while, they will never quite know what it's like to be you, and neither do I. That's why I don't know what you should do.

The third reason I shouldn't give advice, especially to graduates, is that graduates have to sit through any number of ceremonial advice-giving sessions in the first place. Why do we pick on graduates? Granted, their lives are not settled. But whose life is really settled? I constantly hear people exclaim, "If you had told me a year ago that this would be happening to me now, I never would have believed it!" Nobody's life is settled for all time, I am sure of that, and it's the graduates who already get a disproportionate amount of unsolicited advice. Why would a kindly minister want to make matters worse?

The fourth reason I shouldn't give advice to graduates and those making other transitions is that ministers talk too much to begin with. Studies show that 42 percent of churchgoers regularly fall asleep in church. Among those who are able to stay awake, more than one-third of those questioned look at their watch in church every Sunday, and 10 percent shake their watch, thinking it must have stopped. Even though you yourself are reading this, the point is well-taken. Everybody knows that the clergy give too much advice in the first place. Why compound the problem?

I'll tell you why. I'll tell you why someone who didn't graduate from high school, who doesn't really know what you should do, who knows you get too much advice already, and whose job makes her preach too much to begin with, would offer advice nonetheless. It's because you hold such promise. That's why most people give advice: they care about you and they want things to go well for you.

It's my particular business to fuss over you about theological matters.

You may have heard about the Hasidic tradition's "two-pocket theology," the idea that religious people should always have two pockets in every garment, a slip of paper in each one. The first piece of paper should say, "I am but dust and ashes." And the second should say, "For me the universe was made." I want to make sure that as a Unitarian Universalist, you keep both slips of paper handy.

I want you to hear the message about being dust and ashes, about not being self-centered and arrogant. But equally important is the companion theological message: "For me the universe was made," the message about how empowered you are, how terrific you are. And so I offer this piece of advice:

Remember that something inside you is holy, and you are capable and strong, and at the same time, you are interconnected within the universe, and you are small.

There is much more advice to be given, of course, and I can scarcely stop myself: Along the lines of earning your keep, about love, about finding a center or a god or some life of the spirit, about using your head to think things through, about independence and connection. There are ethical rules you need to have at the ready, and expressions of joy, and committed acts. But you know me—I'm not apt to offer advice.

Quiescence

A Hindu prayer begins, "Waters, you are the ones who bring us the life force."

There's something about water. A number of you mention the ocean when you talk about substantive religious experiences. Or sometimes you tell me about dreams you've had, where you float serenely down a warm river. A few of you mention that a hot bath at the end of the day is what calms you, saves you in fact, from the chaos of the day.

And so on this summer day, when our mood may be of "quiescence," I would stay with this drifting feeling, this sense of floating down a river.

Of course, no minister can resist metaphor, so it's difficult to get more than a few words into a sermon without turning the river into symbols of this and that. I will use just one, the most predictable one: the river as a journey through life. You know, "life is like a river." And to do that I'll go to a book about trout fishing by Ted Leeson. The author reflects on an extended fishing trip he's taking:

> You don't take a trip like this. It takes you. It is indeterminate, open-ended, almost a succession of tangents except that there is no main line of navigation and so nothing is really tangential. . . . What you sense most clearly are the currents outside yourself, shifting forces of uncertain direc-

tion. And in such moments, what's needed most is to throw up a sail, pull in the keelboard, and just see where the drift takes you.

Now, nobody's mother—and I am a mother—nobody's mother is going to say, "Honey, you're out of high school now, how's this for a life plan: Why don't you just flow with the currents, go with the shifting forces of uncertain direction, and see where the drift takes you?" No, my general program would include quite the opposite, with an eye to a livable wage, or an extended stint with the semester system.

I am a wife, too, and living the rest of life with the "uncertain drift" plan in a spouse also seems decidedly unappealing. Yet here we have it, dewy-eyed quotations and a homily waxing poetic about meandering rivers.

So I take it back. Drifting rivers may not serve very well as metaphors for life. But drifting rivers can be excellent metaphors for spiritual nurture.

Every one of us seems to need a break from earning that livable wage, or from the semester system, or from the same four walls, or from whatever routine dailiness is. To make that shift, to stop whatever it is we do, to interrupt the usual lives we lead in order to plumb the spiritual depths is not always easy. The *Habit of Rivers* continues:

Traveling like this with no destination and no steam of your own takes some getting used to. It is difficult not to look ahead, not to see yourself on the way to somewhere. . . . For the first few days, I reluctantly picked at the trip like a plate of existential vegetables. I missed my wife, worried about the weather, about work left undone, about where to go next. . . . I waited, bored by my own company, and considered turning back. There seemed to be no point, which was true, and was also precisely the point.

To be alone with our own souls is important, but not always easy, often not fun, and not dependably exciting. In fact, the title of this homily, "Quiescence," came from a line I read in the old book by John P. Marquand called *The Late George Apley*, where the central character says of a soul-searching morning at church, "The hour and a half at Church was a period of complete quiescence and, must I say it frankly, an interval of such boredom as I have never known since."

I understand that people are different, and that for some the idea of drifting, alone, for days or weeks with nothing but trout for company sounds not at all like heaven on earth. You just want out of that boat and into the nearest jazz club or family gathering or golf game.

But, says Ted Leeson,

Unpatterned time and routineless days tug at you with a sly, seductive insistence; bit by bit, they persuade you to themselves and begin to win you over. The ordinary formulae of daily life give way to pleasantly odd private jags, eating when the mood strikes, sleeping when it suits you, fishing or not, abruptly deciding to move on or content to linger, keeping irregular hours. . . .

According to Jung, crossing a river represents a fundamental change of attitude. Pity he didn't fish; he would have recognized that rivers are far more powerful as agents of transformation than symbols for it.

"Rivers are far more powerful as agents of transformation than symbols for it."

So much gets attached to our lives unbidden. I don't know what your agent of transformation is at this time of year, what calms your soul, what revives your life's spirit, what it is that makes you "stop." Maybe it's a rinse in the river, right down to the base of your being; or drifting on it, or trout fishing in it. Maybe you are renewed by a lingering gardening project with your children or a cooling afternoon in a city park. Maybe it is the quiet of this time with a sermon, here and now—the quiescence of this moment—that is a calming presence. Whatever your particular habit, may the life spirit continually find ways to flow back in.

The Doors Slide Open

In the sixth grade there was a boy in my class who had a steel plate in his skull and was always complaining how test answers could never get through to him. Our teacher would say, "Give me a break."

In a way, though, the boy was right. Every human being on the face of the earth has a steel plate in his head, but if you lie down now and then and get still as you can, it will slide open like elevator doors, letting in all the secret thoughts that have been standing around so patiently, pushing the button for a ride to the top. The real troubles in life happen when those hidden doors stay closed for too long. But that's just my opinion.

— *Sue Monk Kidd*, The Secret Life of Bees

You know what they say: Summertime is the time for dreaming, for slowing down to reflect. To be fair, they say that about winter too, when we're supposed to curl up with a cup of cocoa during those long evenings, thinking thoughts of life and death and what it's all about. And wait. Don't they also say that about autumn and spring? But still, for me, summer is the best time to crowbar those steel plates open.

In an old issue of *Harper's* magazine, Edwin Dobb says, "Again and again I drove to the edge of my existence and cocked my ears."

That's what I try to do.

It's the lazy way to gain religious renewal. Not being prone to spiritual practice, I believe I've found the next best strategy—something, as the man says, to do with the edge of existence.

Something to do with transformation, or maybe, to be fair, not really transformation—I'm just shooting for a little improvement in the clarity-of-perspective department.

I get out of my element.

For instance, one year I lucked out. I got on a house-boat in the American Southwest with my family. We were miles and miles from anyone else, from a cell phone signal or Wi-Fi connection, or from any kind of landscape we had ever seen before. When we'd go ashore, we were ignoramuses amid the tumbleweeds (at least we figured those things were tumbleweeds), the red sandstone (no good for climbing, it turned out), the lizards (should we pet them or run for our lives?), and the desert's outrageous thorns (those little buddies have got to hurt). We were utter buffoons when it came to the boat itself, what with its propellers, kilomage, generator, anchors, and choke. We were New Englanders at the edge of what we knew.

And what of spiritual intentionality—the cocked ear? No need out there—as I said, I was taking the lazy way. The beauty was bombastic. The isolation complete. My love for my family fierce. Wonder and awe immediately at hand. In *The Solace of Fierce Landscapes*, David Douglas tells us, "The crops of wilderness have always been its spiritual values—silence and solitude, a sense of awe and gratitude—able to be harvested by any traveler who visits." You bet.

The steel plate slid open easily like elevator doors, no need for the crowbar. And in came all the secret thoughts that had been standing around so patiently—thoughts about groundedness and goodness, thoughts about what needs doing in spite of the vastness and the mystery, thoughts about thankfulness and what counts and what doesn't.

I know, I know—the houseboat thing was a fluky circumstance, and life doesn't often provide so grand a chance for renewal. But I stand by the general point. As the poet Denise Levertov puts it, "If we are to survive the disasters that threaten, and survive our own struggle to make it new—a struggle I believe we have no choice but to commit ourselves to—we need tremendous transfusions of imaginative energy."

Get it when and where you can, the kids and the terrible schedule and work and the price of things notwithstanding. Maybe you are ripe for a spiritual practice. Or a trip across the state. Or a new language, new playlist, or new poet. Maybe it's time to stop with the poets and playlists and whatever else you can think of, join the "slow movement," and create the gaps, the pauses, and the time for "lying down now and then and getting as still as you can." Do whatever it takes to slide those steel plates open like elevator doors, letting in all the secret thoughts. For the real trouble in life happens when those hidden doors stay closed for too long.

Who's to Blame?

I am sitting in a roomful of about forty Polish Catholics. We are in a funeral home, Sobocinski's Funeral Home, "between," as anybody from Detroit would say, "8 and 9 Mile." The occasion is sad, of course, as my husband's father has died, and there he is, in his open casket, right there with us. But most of the people have been in the room for all twelve of the visiting hours, as seems to be their custom, "6–9 Wednesday and 12–9 Thursday," and by this time somehow it is perfectly natural to sit around talking and laughing and remembering.

It's a grand reunion. In the midst of the grieving I am sitting with the aunts and girl cousins; they are telling me that the butcher has begun to put a touch too many prunes in the kielbasa and it's turning out too sweet; they are telling me that their grandchildren won't eat duck blood soup unless they say the brownish soup is chocolate; they are telling me the rosary service is about to start.

I fail the rosary test. They know I'm not Catholic, and not even Polish—some of them boycotted our wedding on that account—but decades have gone by, some of their own children have gone on to marry even worse, and this time they want to make me feel welcome. So what do they say to me? We hear it all the time. They say, "Oh Jane, don't worry. There's only one God."

Well I would have been delighted to get into a little theological discussion right there at Leo Sobocinski's

Funeral Home, but unaccustomed to the funeral customs as I was, even I was pretty sure that that discussion would be inappropriate at that particular location between 8 and 9 Mile, with that particular crowd.

You, on the other hand, are fair game.

In my opinion, human beings do not all believe in the same god. First, it goes without saying that large numbers of people, many among us, take the perfectly tenable position that no god exists at all. But among those who do believe in god, the gods vary dramatically.

One of the Bantu gods, Ndjambi, is an omnipresent, kind god, who sends rain and blessings upon the people, asking nothing in return. A contrasting god, a god on the Labrador Peninsula, the master of the caribou, spends his time watching to see if anybody comes within 150 miles of his home, and if they do, he kills them. A Colombian goddess is seen as the mother of all things—the thunder, the streams, the trees, the sun, and the Milky Way. I am quite certain, had we been able to have the discussion, that the Polish aunts and uncles would agree that these are not the gods that were present at the rosary service at Sobocinski's Funeral Home. We don't all believe in the same god; of that I feel quite sure.

Even the god viewed by Christians and Jews differs in temperament, motivations, and strategies for getting human beings to behave. But during the Jewish High Holy Days, it's worth noting that this god knows how to forgive, knows how to grant mercy. This god doesn't always do it, but has that capacity.

Every year, as Yom Kippur approaches, I find some way to preach about forgiveness. Unitarian Universalists were raised in all manner of religious and nonreligious households, and we've each come to view theology in our own ways. But I think we all care about forgiveness, and so at this time of the year I talk about forgiving ourselves, about forgiving one another, about letting ourselves be forgiven.

But this year I have another angle on forgiveness. This year, I want to talk about forgiving god—whichever of the gods might be yours, if you have one at all. Or forgiving the universe. Making peace with whatever it is that allows bad things to happen—even if it's simply the random and natural way of the world. I want to talk about making peace with the fact that we are witness to atrocities, and that sometimes those atrocities happen to us. I want to talk about how it feels to be angry at god, whichever god that might be.

You may remember that Shakespeare's King Lear, in Act III, having endured estrangement from his daughters, having been dispossessed and displaced and driven to distraction on his way to madness, stands in a storm on the heath and rails at the gods:

> Blow, winds, and crack your cheeks! Rage! Blow!
> You cataracts and hurricanes, spout
> Till you have drench'd our steeples, . . .
> You sulph'rous and thought-executing fires,
> Vaunt-couriers to oak-cleaving thunderbolts,

Singe my white head! And thou, all-shaking
    thunder,
Smite flat the thick rotundity o' the world!
Crack nature's molds. . . .
Let the great gods,
That keep this dreadful [turmoil] o'er our heads,
Find out their enemies now.

That's the feeling I'm talking about. You are beyond the last straw. You didn't deserve this, nobody does. You can't take it anymore, it isn't fair, and you are more than ready to blame whomever's in charge. I'm not talking about reacting to the little day-to-day aspects of life that go wrong—you run out of milk, your good shoes get soaked in the rain, the ATM is out of order, the highway is backed way up. I'm referring to one tragedy heaped upon another tragedy until your spirit is all but broken.

In some religions, you can deliver a bowl of rice to your god and that god will go easy on the disasters for a while. In some religions you can say some special words over and over again and your god will get to feeling friendly to you. In some religions you can kill a chicken or a goat and your god will reward you with good health, or riches, or rain when you need it. You may, yourself, believe in petitionary prayer, or that right living or proper attitude results in god's favor, or that confession or sacrifice or promises will change the course of events. But no matter what our beliefs, whether we believe we can affect the powers that be or we believe in an indifferent universe altogether, we each have to reckon with the fact that no matter what we do, horrible things sometimes happen. It's a profound and universal human experience.

In the Hebrew scriptures, Psalm 22, we read,

My God, my God, why have you forsaken me?
Why are you so far from helping me, from the
words of my groaning?
O my God, I cry by day, but you do not answer;
and by night, but find no rest. . . .
I am poured out like water,
and all my bones are out of joint;
my heart is like wax;
it is melted within my breast;
my mouth is dried up like a potsherd,
and my tongue sticks to my jaws;
you lay me in the dust of death.

Likewise, in the Christian scriptures, Jesus gets into a terrible mess, the unthinkable crucifixion. Over the years of early Christianity, as the story of the crucifixion began to collect the details born of imagination, people speculated about what Jesus might have said as he hung on the cross. The Gospels of Matthew and Mark, though not the others, wound up pasting the beginning of Psalm 22 into the crucifixion story, and so we have Jesus expressing the same, very human sentiment as the psalmist: "My God, my God, why have you forsaken me?"

And don't we know that feeling? God has abandoned

us. Or maybe you would put it not in terms of god but this way: You believe that the cosmos operates according to a generally positive plan, but that plan seems suddenly to have gone haywire. Or maybe you put it down to karma, or past lives. Or maybe you believe that what is, just is, and the chips fall where they may. In any case, how will you cope with that feeling that whatever you had counted on or hoped for has let you down?

If you believe in a conventional god, you have two common choices (though of course there are others). You can say to yourself, "I believe in god, and god is good, but god isn't really in control of everything." Or you can say, "I believe in god, and god is in control of everything, but god has decided that, for whatever reason, we human beings are going to experience the full range of circumstance." As Archibald MacLeish says in his play, *J.B.,*

If God is God He is not good.
If God is good He is not God;
Take the even, take the odd.

You may remember Rabbi Harold Kushner's book, *How Good Do We Have to Be?* In this book, as well as in one of his other best sellers, *When Bad Things Happen to Good People*, Kushner takes the position that the bad things just aren't god's fault. That god loves us and wouldn't be cruel.

On the Christian side, the distinguished theologian from several decades ago, Dietrich Bonhoeffer, winds up in a similar place. He says that god suffers *with* us. God is not all powerful.

Another way of solving the problem of why god lets bad things happen is to say that god is just god, creating life, directing the galaxies, doing god's thing. Good and evil are merely human constructs; god knows nothing about them. You can even cite the Bible for this one if you want to: Jesus says, "God makes His sun rise on the evil and on the good, and sends rain on the just and the unjust."

Those two solutions—where you decide that either god is not all-powerful or god is not all-merciful—are very well for those of you who believe in a more or less conventional god. But the rest of us are left still wondering: How do human beings cope with utter tragedy?

I was recently reminded of an old story about three rabbis. They put god on trial for allowing children to be murdered during the Holocaust. The rabbis went into the temple and held the trial. They found god guilty for this most unspeakable of sins. After the trial, as they came out of the temple, one of the rabbis noticed it was almost sundown. He said to the others, "Look, it is time to pray." And the three rabbis knelt down in prayer.

There it is. That's the answer—an answer worth thinking about for Yom Kippur. The answer to the question, "How do human beings cope when their gods or their universe or their world view has failed them?" That's what people do in one form or another: They forgive god. They come to terms with whatever's in charge: the cosmos, happenstance, god. And then, wonder of wonders, they turn around and find something to praise. They— we—continue to pray or to sing or to note beauty with pleasure. We live on in spite of it all. We smile. We affirm. We find some positives out there.

Earlier, I quoted Psalm 22. But not all of Psalm 22. The writer, the lamenter, rails against god, but in fact he alternates between railing and praising. He complains, but then he goes on to tell god, "I will tell of your name to my brothers and sisters; in the midst of the congregation I will praise you. . . . All the ends of the earth shall remember and turn to the Lord; and all the families of the nations shall worship before him."

That's what two-thirds of the Psalms do: They talk about the horrors of illness, famine, plague, siege, or exile, and then they talk about god's majestic attributes, god's power, and how thankful they feel. Pretty weird, I know, but I think that's what most of us do too, in one form or another. We whine, we put up a major fuss, and then we go out for ice cream. Life is unbearable, and my, didn't that taste good.

I got a book catalog in the mail the other day and I noticed a James Thurber collection entitled *People Have More Fun than Anybody.* That's exactly the conclusion that the psalmist, and most of us, come to. Really awful things happen in our world. Sometimes they happen to us. But still, somehow, mostly we survive—we better than survive, we go on living, and with luck, we forgive whatever powers or circumstances that may be out there, and we get back in touch with the fact that people do have more fun than anybody.

We regain the ability to notice the incredible harvest moon. We laugh out loud at the stupidest line on late-night TV. The September sun feels warm on the top our head. The comfort of a friend is welcome. The turn of phrase in the library book, the melody of a song, strikes us just right. Our beds are warm and cozy. And before we know it, we are living life again, singing praise, looking at a good day ahead. We don't all believe in the same god— we may not believe in any god at all. But during these High Holy Days, we have forgiven whatever's in charge.

The Curse of Columbus

Two hundred years ago, during a spirited debate in Europe, the Academy of Lyons offered a prize of 1,200 francs for the best essay on the topic "Was the discovery of America a blessing or a curse?" A blessing or a curse for them, of course.

The topic, if not the contest, was popular, and scientists and philosophers came to one conclusion: Columbus's conquest of the New World had been the greatest of all misfortunes. They noted that the reptiles and insects in the New World were very large, and the quadrupeds small, and the people cold. They told the world that the Americas were a dank and gloomy land where no birds sing and no dogs bark, a place "so ill-favored by nature that all it contains is either degenerate or monstrous."

Centuries later, though the theory of American biological inferiority has long been relegated to the past, the cursedness, the greatest of all misfortunes, remains—now from the perspective of the indigenous peoples and their allies.

Here's what I wish I could do: I wish I could write about the positive side of Christopher Columbus's contribution to history, and then mention the drawbacks. Nice and balanced. But friends, there is no balancing—those days have been over for decades.

Historians now agree that Columbus was motivated simply by greed, not by the sense of adventure, or a commitment to exploration, or the desire for challenge. In advance of his trip he demanded 10 percent of all the wealth that would ever be discovered for himself and his descendents in perpetuity, he demanded the titles "Viceroy" and "Admiral of the Ocean Sea"—a hereditary title— and that he would be governor of all new territories. Then, off he went, with outdated, inaccurate navigational calculations, to sail the ocean blue. In the course of four trips he reached the Bahamas (though nobody knows quite where), the Greater Antilles, the South American land-mass, and Central America, believing to his death that he had reached Asia. It was all so confusing that at one point, flawed stargazing led him to decide that he had sailed uphill—so says Tony Horwitz in *A Voyage Long and Strange*.

We all know that Columbus showed up on the doorsteps of established homelands and ancient civilizations. As many as eighty million people lived in the Americas at the time. In a letter, Columbus describes one group he encounters this way: "They are very simple and honest and exceedingly liberal with all they have. They exhibit great love toward all others in preference to themselves. . . . I did not find, as some of us had expected, any cannibals among them." So far so good.

But then the horror of this history begins. In *Columbus: His Enterprise* by Hans Koning we read, "With fifty men we could subjugate them all and make them do whatever we want."

And that's what he did. Christopher Columbus initiated the trans-Atlantic slave trade. In 1495, on his second of the four trips, he rounded up 1,500 native people and imprisoned them in pens, guarded by men and dogs. He took the "best" five hundred and loaded them aboard ship. Two hundred died, three hundred arrived at the auction block in Seville. He wrote, "Let us in the name of the Holy Trinity go on sending all the slaves that can be sold." Though he later changed his focus from slavery to gold, reading about Columbus includes pages and pages of graphic brutality.

In 1992, people around the world planned to celebrate the Christopher Columbus Quincentenary Jubilee. Fireworks. Special Exhibits. Documentaries. Souvenirs. Tall ships. It would be grand. But in the face of the upcoming celebration, we all began to confront the truth about the guest of honor. Celebration gave way to repentance and reflection.

So it was, almost two decades ago, that many began to ask the religious questions in earnest. How can we combat racism in the histories we tell? How can we promote justice for indigenous people everywhere? How can we learn the rhythms of the planet and live in harmony? Where does greed get us? How will we use our power? If we are to celebrate, we can begin by celebrating the continued asking of these questions.

Back in 1991, my colleague Rev. David Rankin wrote, "I know . . . it is difficult to swallow. Inside, I want to resist the message. I want to refuse the changed perspective. I want to keep the heroes. A small voice pleads: 'Why not shoot off the fireworks? Why not enjoy the party? What is wrong with pretending?'" And then he goes on to say that there is no pretending. No running away. "I must revise myself, my own mentality, in order for the cycle to end. Crushing our idols is not an easy task."

We are what we celebrate, and genocide, brutality, elitism, and greed are not on the list.

> But there is a progress in naming and facing the truth.
> May we know that progress.
> There is honor in telling the untold story.
> May we know that honor.
> There is hope in claiming a new vision.
> May we know that hope.

The Point of Time Capsules

When my dad was in junior high school, he built a colorful box the size of a small footlocker. In that box he put treasures. And then he bought a padlock and locked it up, vowing not to open the box for twenty-five years. I remember that box from the days when I was young, stashed under the basement stairs, waiting, waiting.

The last years were the longest, but the time did arrive, and miraculously, Dad still knew where the key was. What he didn't know anymore was what was in the box. He was as enthralled as any of us when Mom and we kids gathered around and he opened it up. Comic books, and postcards illustrated with pictures of ships. Marbles. A compass. The letters from camp required a little deciphering, and the Morse Code book and the fish hooks took a good bit of explaining, all to good effect. Several fancily-tied sailor's knots were in the box, and a whittled stick, and metal chess pieces. Getting acquainted with Dad-the-kid was excellent. Even more stunning was the notion of my father having sent a message to himself, announcing what seemed important—his own private time capsule.

That's the point about time capsules.

According to an article I read years ago in *The Atlantic Monthly* magazine, the people in Wilkinsburg, Pennsylvania, decided that to commemorate the community's centennial, the contents of a time capsule buried twenty-five years earlier should be dug up. The exact location didn't seem to be documented anywhere, but eighty-seven-year-old Harold J. Ake, known as "Chick," seemed to recall something about it being underneath the flower beds "down there in front of the railroad station." A day of digging turned up nothing. And it is reported that Chick Ake went home and wrote the following in his diary: "Oh well."

I think that's OK. I think Chick Ake was on the mark when he responded by saying, "Oh well." Because as the author of the article, sociologist Albert Bergesen, points out, the time capsule of Wilkinsburg had probably already fulfilled a purpose. It may not have been a message from one generation to the next, but the capsule had been what it no doubt needed to be: a message from one generation to itself.

I have often been told to focus "on the here and now." So it makes sense to me to launch a here-and-now time capsule—bearing, as Bergesen suggests, a message from one generation to itself. After all, you can buy aluminum time capsules (in matte or satin finish) ready to go—all you have to do is supply the contents.

Which is not so easy. Time capsule commentators judge harshly; they feel disappointed when they unearth a capsule only to find old railway schedules, golf balls, slide rules, newsreels, and maybe a hat. What's the message in a collection like that?

The appropriate exercise is obvious, though tough. What do we value? What objects reflect those values?

What would we cram into, say, 1.7 cubic feet that would make plain our work and our hopes? What do we have to say for ourselves?

I seem to have posited a question that I myself can't quite answer! Let's make it easier. What if we were to tackle this project from the perspective of thanksgiving? What are we grateful for?

Myself, I'd look for a little globe to put in the time capsule, I think, and a photograph of a lot of people—all different kinds—including, of course, my family and friends. And small plant and animal replicas—common and outrageous—feathered, slithery, high jumpers, and something with scales and great big eyes. I'd get started finding the best and most profound poem that I could, or sacred writing. Perhaps something very smart, and outrageously funny as well. I would enclose a love note. For starters.

If there were any cubic feet at all left in the time capsule, it would be important to include a brief message, a summary, in case the values reflected in the conglomeration were not crystal clear. A few good, heartfelt words about how grateful I feel for life itself and all that is dear—along the lines of what one might say when loved ones gather around a Thanksgiving table.

The junior-high version of my dad had the impulse, if not the maturity, to encapsulate the precious, so as not to lose track of it as the unimaginable future unfolded. Great as the box was sitting there under the stairs for all that time, Dad didn't really need it—he always knew what he valued. Had the box disappeared over the years, I think he would have said, "Oh well," with the sure knowledge that he had received the message to himself about knowing the treasures in life.

After all, that's the point of time capsules. And Thanksgiving.

The Full Pilgrim Treatment

The Mayflower, . . . now numbering one hundred and two souls, left Plymouth September 16th, 1620, and began its historic journey westward. For a goodly part of the voyage of over two months' duration the ship was buffeted by equinoctial winds and high seas . . . After a long beating at sea they fell with that land which is called Cape Cod, . . . and they were not a little joyful. . . .

It was the 21st of November when the Mayflower dropped anchor in the sheltered and quiet waters of Provincetown Harbor and one may well imagine the happiness and gratitude of these weary voyagers when they sighted this haven of refuge and were once more able to place their feet upon dry land. As Bradford records: "Being thus arrived in a good harbor and brought safe to land, they fell upon their knees and blessed the God of heaven who had brought them over the vast and furious ocean, and delivered them from all the perils and miseries thereof, again to set their feet on the firm and stable earth, their proper element."

—*William Atwood, "The Pilgrim Story"*

I got the full Pilgrim treatment in elementary school: construction paper Pilgrims in the windows of the school—their little faces made from the stack of pink paper, the shoes from the black pile, and the buckles made out of the yellow-colored paper. We made Pilgrim hats for ourselves, too—black paper hats complete with the now familiar yellow buckles. Finally, for our last artistic history project, we'd trace our hands, color the fingers to look like feathers, and call the result a turkey.

So I knew about Pilgrims from school: Pilgrims crowded together on the Mayflower, they landed, said hello to the Indians, and they all ate one heck of a Thanksgiving dinner. That was the basic deal on Pilgrims when I was growing up.

All this loses its appeal once you know the true history. We grow up, we stop tracing our hands to make the holiday turkeys, we go for years without giving the Pilgrims the time of day, we leave it all behind.

So this year I thought I'd go another round with the Pilgrims.

A pilgrim is a person who travels from place to place, a person who journeys. A wanderer. The nineteenth-century poet Dante Gabriel Rossetti defined *pilgrim* as anyone who "leaveth the place" of his or her birth.

I had always thought that a pilgrim was on some kind of a religious trip, or that the word was used as a metaphor for an important quest of the sort I myself would never think of embarking upon. The word pilgrim was used by pious types who knew about higher purposes than mine. But really, dictionary-definition pilgrims, pilgrims without the capital "P," are just folks like me, like most of us. Folks who once were born and from that point on, began wandering through life.

Most of the time we put one foot in front of the other just fine. But now and then, like the famous Pilgrims in the opening quotation, we step onto a boat that does get "buffeted by equinoctial winds and high seas," and then as weary voyagers we, like they, sight our haven of refuge and put our feet upon dry land once more. As Governor Bradford said, "again we set our feet on the firm and stable earth, their proper element."

We do wander through life. I guess that makes us pilgrims. We're moving along and boom. The measles. Boom. A home run. Boom. We're in love. Boom. Somebody dies. Boom. We get what we thought we wanted. Boom. That wasn't quite it. Boom. Life is clear. Boom. No it isn't. We are pilgrims. We travel from place to place.

In a poem by Galway Kinnell called "Middle of the Way," the narrator wanders around in the snow, loses the trail, finds it, stumbles around in the dark, eventually relies on a map and compass, and finally warms himself by a comforting fire. He says,

> All I see is that we float out
> Into the emptiness, among the great stars,
> On this little vessel without lights. . . .
> Half my life belongs to the wild darkness.

I find that enormously comforting. I like knowing that we pilgrims don't always have to have a New World ahead, or even a destination. Pilgrims can, if we want to, just float out into the emptiness, among the great stars, on a little vessel without lights. I like knowing that floating around in the "wild darkness" is a legitimate cosmic game plan.

227

I understand that most of us pilgrims do our best to keep gas in the car and breakfast cereal lined up on the shelf; we try to get the trash out on the right day, have a matched pair of clean socks in the drawer, and know where our keys are. We don't notice the floating so much that way, or the darkness. We are pilgrims, short on buckle shoes perhaps, but pilgrims. The truth is, we don't know the route, exactly—even though we do our best to map it out. We're going to have to wander and float. Those equinoctial winds are going to get us sometimes, but most of the time, the firm and stable earth is right there up ahead. We are pilgrims, traveling from place to place. And I, for one, am going to enjoy the trip.

The Mystery of Christmas Past

The middle of December. I know what it's like. I know what goes on. The time has come. You bundle up, start the car, and drive in the drizzle over to the mall. You can't find a parking place. Finally you spot somebody—a fellow walking to his car—and slowly you follow him as he wanders around the parking lot, drifting from aisle to aisle, lane to lane, until he finally finds his car, fumbles with his packages and car keys, gets in, smokes a cigarette, and vacates the parking space.

Why are you in single-minded pursuit of this space? You need this parking space because two thousand years ago, a baby was born in a stable.

The store is crowded. It's 30 percent off, plus the 10 percent off coupon you hope you really did put in your pocket on your way out the door. You purchase the percolator for your mother-in-law even though, as it turns out, the 30 percent off does not apply to "small appliances" and the coupon wasn't in your pocket after all. You harvest a number of Christmas presents, a baby doll—"Baby Wiggles and Giggles" to be precise—an electronic dart board, a large bottle of rum, a gingerbread house with M&Ms on it, a chain saw, an oversized tin can of caramel and cheese-flavored popcorn, and some gift bags with illustrations of Rudolph the Red Nosed Reindeer on them. Oh, and an inexpensive Grinch wristwatch for yourself, and a red sweater, too, for those parties coming up.

Why are you buying the reindeer bags and the chain saw and the gingerbread house? You spend your money and your time on percolators and popcorn because— well, because once upon a time, it is told, a wrinkled little baby was born to a mother named Mary.

Back in the car, you're off to buy your Christmas tree. The lot is full of trees. Short trees, tall trees, medium trees. For the life of you, suddenly you just can't picture the height of your own living room ceiling. You take a guess, drag the tree over to the register and pay for it, and only then wonder how in the world you'll get the darn thing home. Should have thought of that before. So you borrow some twine, drive the tree home on the roof of the car, wrestle it into the stand, untangle all those lights, exclaim at how many are burned out, and begin the desperate annual training maneuvers for your cat and dog, who never remember the Christmas tree rules from year to year.

Why did you bring a full-fledged spruce into your living room and wind a couple of strings of electric light bulbs around it? You put a tree in your house with lights on it because, you see, two thousand years ago, there was this baby born in a desert town far, far away. And you are celebrating.

Whew. You're tired. But you keep on going. You roll out the dough, nicely chilled by now, and you cut it into cookie shapes. A bell. A camel. A star. A bow. A snowman. A round Santa Claus. Another camel. Another bell. Over and over again until the dough is warm and sticky and small, even what with all that flour.

At last you sit at the kitchen table and have a drink of eggnog. The holiday music is on: "I Saw Mommy Kissing Santa Claus," "Let It Snow, Let It Snow, Let It Snow," and a snappy little medley that includes something about three ships, holly and ivy, bells that jingle, and bringing a torch. Why are you baking snowman cookies to further tunes of drumming boys and midnights clear? You are singing and baking because, along about two thousand years ago, that baby was born as the animals watched, and this is how you recognize that. Not you literally— you yourself may stay away from malls, Rudolph, and cookie dough. You may celebrate different holidays altogether—but plenty of people do celebrate this way in December.

Do you ever wonder what happened to the good old days, when the connection to Jesus at Christmas was strong, where the horse drew the sleigh, and the tree was trimmed with cranberries and popcorn and simple homemade ornaments? Where you gave an orange as a present, or a hair ribbon? Where you sat by the fire surrounded by a large and loving family, ate your Christmas pudding, and sang "God Rest Ye Merry Gentlemen"? Have you ever wanted to replicate the days gone by when the spiritual meaning of Christmas was first and foremost, and economic indicators were completely unheard of?

I hope not, because those days never existed. When we wax nostalgic about the uncomplicated days when the spiritual aspects of Christmas prevailed, those days before Christmas went commercial, those temperate days when Christmas was religious and pure—we are dreaming—making it all up.

Christmas didn't really get going in the United States until the mid-1800s, and at that point Americans created their own holiday. From the beginning, Christmas celebrations were about merriment and presents and food and songs and cards and getting together and making money and buying frivolous decorations. From the very beginning Americans put together whatever they felt like putting together, and we've called that hodgepodge "Christmas."

So what we have is some people making strudel in celebration of Christmas, and some ordering poinsettias, and some creating a nativity scene in the front yard, and others building a doll house for a grandchild. A few folks send a heap of Christmas cards. Some drive around and look at lights, others sing Christmas carols up and down the street. Some eat the cookies that the other people bake—somebody's got to do it—others take children to visit Santa.

It may be just as important to mention that nobody does everything. I am certain that some among us do not shop for or receive presents. Most don't bother with cards. I know that there are people who have a terrible sinking feeling that they might get roped into going to the Nutcracker again this year, but usually they get out of it. Many have never ever baked a Christmas cookie. Lots don't socialize with family—maybe with anybody at all. Plenty of people give up on the Christmas tree, and are quite content to take or leave any number of Christmas customs, or, quite frankly, the whole ball of wax. But still, Christmas is out there, there's no denying that.

I'm pretty sure that ministers are supposed to be able to observe all the Christmas commotion, to look at popular culture in December—the elves and the manger and the figgy pudding—and discern the true meaning of Christmas. It's probably in my contract. And nobody thinks that ministers should be allowed to proclaim that the true meaning of Christmas has to do with shopping and partying and decorating and eating. But the horrible truth is, historically speaking, I think that might be it. Reveling, not religious piety, may be our heritage.

Let's go way back. In the fourth century, the Roman Church had a problem. Officially, the Church wanted to say that Jesus was God. But a sizable minority, our own direct theological ancestors, the ancient Arians, believed that Jesus was entirely human. The Church was beginning to promote the idea of the Trinity, and we did not go along with it.

The Arians—we—did eventually lose that battle, but along the way we were enough of a threat that the official church felt it politic to throw us a bone, and that bone was to admit that Jesus had at least been born just as a human being is born.

So Jesus got to have a birthday. The actual date, of course, slipped all over the calendar for a while, until another bone needed to be thrown—this time to the pagans. The pagan celebrations had persisted in spite of the best efforts of the Church, so the Church decided to set the date of Jesus' birthday celebration during Saturnalia and the winter solstice, when Romans were feasting and reveling anyway. Right at that point, in the early 300s, is when the sacred first tried to interject itself into the annual celebration. But mostly, it didn't work out. The people wanted to party.

We can follow the Christmas festivities over the centuries up into Scandinavia by the sixth century, where they fused with the pagan Norse feast season known as Yule; by the eleventh century the celebrating had traveled into England. By the seventeenth century, the English were dancing, sporting, card playing, gambling, and feasting on Christmas, and they provided one another with elaborate pageants for further entertainment. To be sure, the Church continued its fervent hope that Christian piety would overtake the profane customs of Christmas. Nonetheless, the true meaning of Christmas persisted, and that true meaning can be summed up in the phrase "eat, drink, and be merry."

Now. Enter the Puritan reformers in England, who condemned the Christmas revelers as "hel hounds" in a "Deville's daunce" of merriment. One Puritan writer asks, "Into what a stupendous height of more than pagan impiety . . . have we not now degenerated!" He believed that Christmas ought to be "rather a day of mourning than rejoicing," not a time spent in "amorous mixt, voluptuous, unchristian, that I say not pagan, dancing, to God's, to Christ's dishonour, religion's scandal, chastities' shipwracke and sinne's advantage."

Before we know it, the Puritans crossed the ocean and ruled the Massachusetts Bay Colony, and sure enough, in 1659, Christmas was outlawed. Cotton Mather said, "Can you in your consciences think that our holy saviour is honored by mirth, by long eating, by hard drinking, by lewd gaming, by rude revelling . . . ? Shall it be said that at the birth of our Saviour . . . we take the time to please the hellish legions and to do actions that have much more of hell than of heaven in them?" In the U.S., the Christmas celebrations got off to a slow start.

Time goes by. People from all over Europe show up in America with their Christmas customs. The picture isn't pretty, though, the way it plays out. On Christmas, young rowdies took to the streets and went "wassailing," that is to say they laid siege to the homes of the well-off, demanding free drink and food in a menacing game of trick or treat. In Boston, first the Universalists, then the Unitarians, opened their church doors on Christmas in the hope of calming things down, but that experiment failed.

In the mid-1800s, American culture changed. We had roads and railroads, a national mail system, magazines, and city life. People longed for the simple life, they were impatient with the street reveling on Christmas, so they inadvertently invented a new kind of Christmas: "innovative nostalgia," one scholar calls it. Christmas trees— not that you cut down in the woods, but that you bought in town. Christmas dinner. Stores open till midnight for shopping. Store-bought Christmas cards with the message printed right on them. Carols, hot off the press, that sounded traditional. Store-bought Christmas tree ornaments. Santa Claus gets invented. Magazines publish articles on how to prepare a "traditional Christmas." Churches begin to want a piece of the action—even they begin to decorate for Christmas.

Unitarians got into the act: Charles Dickens, a Unitarian in England, wrote *A Christmas Carol*. Unitarian minister Edmund Hamilton Sears wrote the carol, "It Came Upon the Midnight Clear," the first carol with a social-ethical message, unheard of at the time. "Peace on earth and good will," people said, "just the sort of thing you would expect from a Unitarian."

The list of Unitarian contributions goes on and on: John Bowring wrote "Watchman, Tell Us of the Night," and Henry Wadsworth Longfellow wrote "I Heard the Bells on Christmas Day." Charles Follen, the minister in East Lexington, Massachusetts, introduced the Christmas tree to New England, and James Pierpont wrote "Jingle Bells."

The point is, all along, people have invented their Christmas. We have established what we need to establish to get through the winter. There's no way for any of us to do Christmas "right." We don't have to do all of Christmas. We don't have to worry that by enjoying our friends and families, or by decorating and buying and baking, we're missing out on the true meaning of Christmas. We don't have to worry that somehow we've lost the spiritual essence of Christmas, because Christmas never had a pre-packaged spiritual essence in the first place—we develop that ourselves.

For each one of us, the Christmas we have is the Christmas we choose: the quiet holiday alone with the candle and the passage from Luke, the crazy bustle where you travel a lot of miles and enter the chaos of feasting with family or friends, the Christmas volunteering at a shelter, the Christmas with little children, the Christmas ignored—or so decked out that even the dog wears a big red bow. We keep the customs; we create the heritage.

Why do we buy the gigantic can of caramel popcorn and the percolator and "Baby Wiggles and Giggles"? Because coffee and popcorn and baby dolls could make a loved one happy. And love can be a part of Christmas.

Why do we install a Christmas tree in an apartment that's already too small, decorated with this and that and lights all around? Because it's pretty and fun and the tree lights the darkness. And lighting the darkness can be a part of Christmas.

Why do we knock ourselves out baking cookies in the shapes of stars and singing carols that highlight new baby life and peace and joy? Because we love to hope, and hope can be a part of Christmas.

Love, light, and hope. A fine Christmas indeed.

Still in the Game

I read a newsletter column by one of our Unitarian Universalist ministers in Salt Lake City, Rev. Tom Goldsmith, that I liked a lot. He describes a basketball player named Walter, a clear second-string player of enormous girth, unknown reputation, and ill-fitting shorts. The crowd had come to the game to see Mitch, the star, but Mitch fouled out early on. Thus Walter.

Walter played his heart out, once he overcame his bewilderment at being in the game at all. He jumped "as high as angels fly" in order to retrieve the ball, and the crowd loved him. He was really something!

Tom reminds us at the end of his column that saviors don't all look alike, that sometimes great gifts do come in large packages, and that there are miracles in all of us.

That got me thinking about my own holiday message and three of my own conclusions with respect to Walter and the basketball court.

Point one. Sometimes, we don't live up to the stereotype. We aren't seven feet tall, most of us; and we aren't scoring any points. But still, there we are on the court, in the game, running around, jumping as high as we can, and that turns out to be more than enough.

In the holiday game, we may not have the presents completely under control, or maybe it's the food part, or the holiday cards still in cellophane, but we're still in the game. We have plenty of time to make one person happy with an extra smooch, or a phone call, or a trip around the block to see the Christmas lights or the night sky. Whatever we can do usually turns out to be more than enough. It worked for Walter on the basketball court, and it works for us during the holidays.

Some of us, though, are still on the bench. We get to feeling that we're in a rut. Nothing to do with the holidays especially, it's more the general time of year. It's dark. It's cold. We feel as if we're second string. Nothing's happening. We're twenty-three years old, or forty-two, or sixty-eight, or eighty-eight, and we still haven't made our millions or achieved the perfect family life or written a best seller or found the career that suits us best. It's diaper upon diaper, or another unwelcome foreign post, or the same old grind at work, or we're a little scared that time is running out.

Point two is that the message of "Walter" kicks in, although we're more accustomed to calling it "the holiday spirit." The message is that we get another chance. The new baby Jesus is born with outrageous wonders in store. We can take that good news to heart and if we want to, we get a new life of our own, we get into the game in some new way, energized, hopeful, renewed. The Hanukkah story is the story of another miraculous chance—same with the solstice. We are in the game again, and we run and we jump, and maybe we never shoot the winning basket. In fact, we may not score two points, but what a game we're playing, and how good it feels.

Point three is about miracles—the kind that happen every day—the unlikeliness of the good things that happen to each one of us. We know what the chances were for Walter of capturing the hearts of the fans, but a new day dawned for him, and the fans just loved him.

We're on the receiving end of that kind of luck too— all of us are. For one thing, for those of us in the Northern Hemisphere, the days get shorter and shorter. And shorter. And then, in an unlikely move, on an ordinary day like today, the days will get longer. Even though the sunrise will be no earlier than the day before, the sunset will be later.

The solstice will arrive. For every one of us, the sun will come around again with its new light, just like that. New light. New spirit.

So I like the piece about Walter on the basketball court. It's a good reading for this time of year, for a day like today when we're ready to acknowledge the miracles, the promise, the spirit, and the liveliness of the season. It's holiday time, bathed in new light, and we, each one of us, are in the game.

If Santa Could Talk to Us

If Santa could talk to us as December approaches . . .

- ∽ Wouldn't he tell us he's pretty tired of all the magazine articles about perfect Hanukkah and Christmas gifts for everyone on the list? He's been around, just as we have. He knows it can't be done.

- ∽ Wouldn't he be bored to tears by now with the sermons on the excesses of commercialism? Santa knows the hype's out of control—that's very old news. He's heard that message—just as we have.

- ∽ Wouldn't Santa roll his eyes at the TV segments on the deplorable violence being sold in the toy department? Santa's smart enough to give nice presents, just as we are. Tell him something he doesn't know.

- ∽ Wouldn't he throw up his hands at the stack of advertising fliers and catalogs in his recycling pile? He's got enough paper in his life, thank you very much, just as we do. He doesn't look at any of it, and he's Santa Claus!

～ Wouldn't Santa say, "Hey, the elves and I do this job all year long, and even we don't make it such a big deal." "Relax," he'd say, "it's only presents. Just remember three things":

1. The first thing Santa would probably say is "Giving presents is an excuse for a good time!" That's the first thing. The only reason to give a present is because you want to. You have the chance to focus on what it is that's likable, or even lovable, about a person in your life. You get to recall the moments you've seen the person happy.

You can imagine gift-giving scenarios: You treat that older neighbor (who doesn't drive) to a trip to the planetarium—you both do love the night sky. He's usually pretty crusty, but you can tell: Today, in spite of himself, he's happy. Or you buy your grown-up daughter the complete paperback set of Sue Grafton mysteries. How glad she is! A baby in your life is teething—a wooden spoon, sanded smooth. Bliss. The mother of your children? Wow! A photograph. (She does love her photo albums. She always says that's what she'd grab if the house were on fire.) A photograph of all three kids looking human and happy and everything. She says, "Nice going." You had the foresight to record every single episode of that crazy obscure TV show before it was too late. Your niece and nephew in San Antonio are enraptured, and incidentally, stunned by your good taste.

At holiday time, you can focus on the people you like best or the people for whom you can make a difference.

You have the opportunity to think about what they'd like to receive in combination with what you'd have fun giving. And that's a good deal. Isn't that what Santa would say?

Of course Santa may never have found himself in that perpetual motion machine where they give and so you give and so they give and so you give, and after all, she is your father's only sister, even if she has atrocious taste and inevitably sends you a bag of walnuts, which she knows full well you're allergic to. Santa doesn't stick around long enough on Christmas morning to know what it's like when you've tried, you've really tried, to find something your aunt will appreciate, only to watch her face sag with disappointment year after year, because the only thing she really wants is a delicate hand gun, and frankly, what with your Unitarian Universalist value system, you disapprove. Santa may never have had an aunt like that. But surely he would stroke his whiskers at the prospect and say, "You know, that set-up doesn't make any sense. What are you going to do about it?" The point is, giving presents is an excuse for a good time—yours and theirs.

2. If Santa could talk to us, I think he would say that "Presents are just presents." You can only guess what the giver meant by it. You receive a Brooks Brothers blazer in the mail from your grandmother. Maybe it means, "I love you so much and you're such a handsome guy and I know how you love Brooks Brothers blazers, so Happy Hanukkah." Or maybe it means, "You're such a slob, you never will learn how to dress like a grown-up, but I'm

giving you this blazer, and since you don't make very much money I know you'll have to wear it, and then you'll look more like what I want you to look like. Merry Christmas!" Or how about, "I never was a very good grandmother to you, and now you're all grown up, so I'm sending you this expensive blazer even though I'm living on a fixed income established in 1987, and I hope you'll visit me soon."

Presents can be about control, or indebtedness, or guilt, or competition, or disrespect. They can be about forgiveness, or good cheer, or love, or light-hearted goofiness, or hope for the future of the relationship. One popular book tries to convince us, "Gifts speak for you. Each gift you present becomes an extension of your taste, a measure of your interest in the recipient, even an indication of your personal power. Gift giving can be the key to a successful business relationship, add deeper meaning to a romance, bring joy to your loved ones and warmth to any celebration."

Wouldn't Santa say "No, that doesn't sound too healthy"? Wouldn't Santa say that the proper approach to giving presents is to load up a sleigh with gifts that the folks on the list would enjoy? Wouldn't he suggest happily giving the presents away with a great and loving Santa-esque smile on your face, expecting nothing in return (well, maybe a cookie or two and a glass of milk) and hope that the Legos are received as Legos, and the necklace as a necklace, and the subscription to *National Geographic* as a magazine with especially pretty pictures.

Wouldn't Santa recommend that if you have a message to give, or a message you think you're receiving, to rely on words, nice and clear, and let the presents be presents?

3. Finally, if Santa could talk to us I think he might pick up the phrase that many of us saw in a piece by Rev. Stephen Edington years ago. The article was about gift giving among Native Americans in Massachusetts when the Puritans first landed. In that Indian culture, a gift, once received, was to be given away again. The gift must always move. The gift must always move.

Did somebody teach you to bowl? An older brother, or the nun back at St. Mary's who took a special interest in you, or that very old flame? Well, that gift has to move. You love bowling. Who will you share that with? You've inherited your great-grandmother's handkerchief, the one she brought over on the boat from Latvia. It's in the attic, or the basement—has been for years. But the gift must always move. Who else might appreciate the history, the ties, the roots?

Who are you going to teach to sing "O Come, O Come Emmanuel," or dance the cha-cha, or read *20,000 Leagues Under the Sea*? Who's next in line to receive a flaming chalice necklace? Or the menorah you used as children? The wind-up toys. The Amish crèche. The gift, the really good gift, must always move.

The holidays are approaching, sure as I'm standing here. We know what's in store. We know how to do the holidays.

We're going to be fine. Just remember three things:

1. Giving presents is an excuse for a good time!

2. Presents are only presents.

3. The gift must always move.

If Santa could talk to us, that's what I think he'd say.

Meditation on Winter Holidays

It doesn't get any darker than it gets about now. We sit here on our little planet; tilted into darkness and cold. The night is too long. And too cold.

So if we're Northerners, we do what people did in ancient times, long before churches and pews, long before Santa, long before Jesus, long before Hanukkah: We kindle a flame when the dark is darkest.

Already we are celebrating. And then we add Hanukkah. And so, according to the Jewish calendar, at the waning of the moon nearest the winter solstice, when sun and moon abandon us all, the time is right to light the Menorah, as we make our way out of the darkness.

Thus we add the victory of Judah Maccabee during the second century before the Common Era. Remembering the rededication of the temple, the story of the miraculous oil, we imagine the eight days of hope, born of despair. Eight days of light in the midst of spiritual darkness. We light the Menorah, that the spirit of freedom and miracle may burn for everyone.

Still we are celebrating as we add another story, the story of a baby. Brand new. Flesh and blood. All wrinkled up. The Christmas baby Jesus. Who knew what would happen? All kinds of stories. The baby sneezed. Would he be wondrous? The baby cried. Would he save us all? The baby chortled. Miracle of miracles, a baby who taught us that the human spirit can do great things. That love is worth lifting up. In the coldest part of the year, we added a baby, that we might celebrate our deepest love.

We are celebrating the coming light, the miracles, the baby, and so we drag a tree in, and candles, and latkes. Ding Dong Merrily we go see Santa, we string up those lights and the holly and the ivy, we eat and we greet and we give and we receive that we might feel hope and joy and all good spirits. All best wishes of the season.